FROM PARALYSIS TO PRAISE

THE STORY OF THE NOAH'S ARK MINISTRY

by Shirley Thrush
compiled and edited by
Jerry Thrush, MD

God Bless
Shirley Thrush

From Paralysis To Praise

The Story of the Noah's Ark Ministry

Shirley Thrush

compiled and edited by
Jerry Thrush, M.D.

Essence
PUBLISHING

Belleville, Ontario, Canada

From Paralysis to Praise
Copyright © 2010, Shirley Thrush

Scripture quotations marked KJV are from *The Holy Bible, King James Version*. Copyright © 1977, 1984, Thomas Nelson Inc., Publishers. • Scripture quoataions marked NRSV are from the *New Revised Standard Version* of the Bible, copyright 1989, by the Division of Christian Education of the National Council of the Churches of Christ in the United States of America, and are used by permission. All rights reserved.

ISBN: 978-1-55452-585-0

To order additional copies, visit:
www.essencebookstore.com

For more information, please contact:
Shirley Thrush
411 Safari Rd.
Winston, OR 97496
www.noahsarkwinston.com

Essence Publishing is a Christian Book Publisher dedicated to furthering the work of Christ through the written word. For more information, contact: 20 Hanna Court, Belleville, Ontario, Canada K8P 5J2. Phone: 1-800-238-6376. Fax: (613) 962-3055.
E-mail: info@essence-publishing.com
Web site: www.essence-publishing.com

Printed in Canada
by

Essence
PUBLISHING

DEDICATION

I dedicate this book to my family: to my husband Irvin, who has shared my life's path for the last 55 years; to our two sons Terry and Jerry; and to my grandmother, Teresa Mosier, who told me stories about Jesus when I was a child.

CONTENTS

PROLOGUE

People often ask about what led me, with my husband, to build a replica of Noah's Ark in a small town in Oregon. They inquire about how we came to put a life-sized copy of the Tabernacle of Moses inside, populated with animated characters that share the story of salvation. And they want to understand the source of my deep faith and the roots of the creative process that worked together to develop our ministry here at Noah's Ark.

I have shared the story of parts of my life in various testimonials in churches and meetings. These portions of my story that I have laid open so far have been small glimpses of the whole. To this point, I have felt that many of my life's struggles were too personal or too painful to share. The time is right for releasing my entire testimony with all of its pain and trials.

Our ministry here at Noah's Ark did not begin with a loud voice from the heavens and a command to build an ark as it might have for Noah. It began when I was a small girl, separated from my family, looking death in the eye for the first time as a quadriplegic victim of what was then called infantile paralysis.

It is only through our God, His loving Son, His everlasting Holy Spirit, and the protection by His mighty angels that I have been able to survive these exceptional trials, to raise a family, and to create this ministry. As I will remind you, the ministry is not really mine at all—all things are owned by Him. I believe we are but travelers on our own pathway in this world. All things, even life itself, are temporarily borrowed from above and never owned.

In this story, I will share with you the fire that tempered my soul, the tribulations that strengthened my faith, and the difficult times through which I was carried by our Savior. My faith started small, like a tiny seed, and grew through the years into a mighty tree able to withstand both floods and droughts. It is a faith that became a vision and a vision that became a ministry.

Editor's Note

This book was written to communicate the amazing account of my mother's life and the Noah's Ark Ministry she and my father created in Oregon over the last decade. In it you will discover the foundation of her profound faith, the considerable trials that shaped her, the origins of her ideas for the Noah's Ark Ministry, many of which came from her family, and her personal quest for understanding the Bible. In it I have organized her thoughts and memories into a readable and enjoyable volume.

The story is real. Telling it is limited only by the memory of my mother and my ability to organize and edit her recollections. She is truly thankful to those who influenced her life and to the many volunteers who have helped her create her ministry. She wished to thank each one by name. I regret that this was not possible because of the limitations of human recall, the ability to contact and obtain permission for name use for all involved, and my own editorial talents. Please note that some dialogue has been recreated to illustrate true events and bring them to life.

There is one additional disclaimer that I must make: Material about me must be considered in its context.

Parents like to see their own children portrayed as super-heroes, and my mother is no different. While I did indeed leave high school without a diploma, and I did graduate from college and begin medical school at age nineteen, I was also the child who waded with the sea turtles and ran through the flamingo enclosure at Sea World when the attendants weren't looking. Furthermore, I must confess that I did indeed turn the family motor home into both a train and a boat. Finally, please accept my apologies for any editorial errors or omissions: I accept full responsibility for them. I hope you enjoy reading the book as much as I have editing it!

I wish to thank Jack and Aileen Scharn and Petra LaVictoire, for helping me check for errors, and my son Tristan, who generously donated innumerable hours of his irreplaceable childhood while I worked on this project.

Jerry Thrush, MD

INTRODUCTION: THE SEEDS OF FAITH

As I gaze thoughtfully into the embers of time, the breeze of my thankfulness sparks memories. These memories, effervescent gems that they are, flare up like the flame that has tempered my life. With recollection renewed, they brighten and sparkle with kaleidoscopic brilliance, each portion reflecting the beauty of the other, until the whole becomes a work of art. Art that is life, breathed by the Father through His Son.

I was a little girl who played with homemade dolls and dressed my pets in clothes. I ran barefoot gamboling in the humid Minnesota summers and snuggled under blankets in winters when the Arctic wind blew. My barefoot, carefree, patched-clothes existence forever changed when the loan against optimism was called by soldiers in Europe and viruses at home.

It was a time when hope was borrowed from earth by a world at war. Evil was loosed upon us in form of leaders with the disease of conflict in their hearts—and by microbes with no hearts at all. At that time, there was no jail that could hold the men who did the globe harm, nor cure for many of the diseases that imprisoned children.

Polio raged in our backyard while war seethed in Europe. During the dark time when World War II was on the front stage of the world, backstage, tens of thousands of innocent children from all walks of life were being herded like livestock into prisons of hospitals and sanitariums. The guileless children were not of any specific class, caste, religion, or ethnic background. All were subject to the ravages of the virus regardless of color, creed, or financial status.

In our age of vaccinations and public health, we have little memory of such days of horror and misery. But such recollection, like memories of the wickedness of war, must not fade, or we might overlook the importance of vaccinations—or forget to be wary of smooth-talking leaders with evil in their hearts. If such memory is lost, we will no doubt relive our past.

This book begins in a different era. It was a time before television, before the computer took over our lives, and prior to the invasion of cell phone texting into the space between two individuals standing in the same room. It was an era before astronauts walked on the moon and an age that preceded nuclear weapons, which killed tens of thousands in the name of peace. It was also an epoch that came before our present scourge—terrorist attacks on the west. But, by the grace of God and for His service, I was a survivor and not a statistic. My life was spared that I might be a humble witness for the One who gave life through His sacrifice for us. This is my story and the story of the Noah's Ark Ministry. It is also the story of my family and the others who, with our loving Savior, made it all possible. Walk with me as I share my journey from *Paralysis to Praise*.

TAKEN CAPTIVE BY THE ENEMY IN 1941

The fields and forests of rural Minnesota retain their natural beauty no matter how sizzling the summer or how frigid the winter. In the early 1940s, war brewed in Europe but peace reigned supreme in the pastoral backwaters of America. Our family was close in those faraway farmland days, and although we were not blessed with material possessions, we enjoyed the love of relations and friendship of neighbors. When I was a small child living in the country, a rare but delightful pleasure was a visit to my grandmother who lived in the big city, a half-day trip away. A journey to her house in Minneapolis was a treat of biblical proportions. She was my special friend.

Six decades have passed, but some memories linger as fresh as last week. As a kindergartener, I found the trips to grandmother's house nothing short of magical. The big city was an enchanting place for a little girl from the country. And my grandmother was so much fun! We baked cookies, played with dolls, and she told me stories about a king named Jesus who was born poor like me and who walked on the earth a long time ago.

The excitement was non-stop on one special trip to see my grandmother when I was six, until the morning

I awoke and found that my head seemed to weigh a thousand pounds. I remember the day well. My neck drew back and I began to sway. Suddenly it was hard to breathe. As I struggled to keep my face above my collar, my chest became tight and I knew something was very wrong. Even my grandmother, my favorite sylph of a woman with the faith to move mountains, was helpless to make me better. So she took me to the hospital.

The day they put me in the infirmary was the most terrifying of my short existence. It was a horror that took the shape of formless corridors, echoing walls, and white ceilings for skies. It was a nightmare from which I would not awake for almost a year. When we arrived at the hospital, my first memory was being wheeled down the hall away from my family.

The squat nurse with the rotten-apple nose covered my head with a sheet and dutifully pushed my gurney away from my grandmother. I was too weak to remove the feathery bedcovering from my head let alone sit up and glance back at her. The cacophony of the lobby was replaced by rhythmic squeaking of wheels and the clickety-clack of heels.

The next thing I remember on that day was the image of the nurse's nose as the linen closed like a cavernous mouth over my eyes. I'm sure that her nose wasn't as ugly as I recall, but it was the last thing I saw as the bedding was thrown over my head. My cry, mingled with footsteps and talking wheels, echoed along the corridor. I squealed with all the terror a child could unleash as the nurse took me away.

My mind went blank, and I began to cry. I was unable to escape the prison of my gurney. I knew I was as weak as a kitten overdosed on milk and powerless to get back home to the likes of cookies and dolls. I realized that I couldn't fight back. It took all my effort to breathe. Screaming was as exhausting as it was useless, so I soon gave up on that too.

Oh, how I wanted to run away down the corridor and out the door. If I couldn't do that, how I wanted just to be able to sit! But I couldn't as much as hold up my head. The pillow held my head in place as if it were a magnet on metal. The nurse began to explain why she put the sheet over my head, and her clarification fueled the fire of panic rather than quelling it.

"Bugs," said the nurse as she carted me down the hall. "I don't want to get your bugs." Although she no doubt meant microbes, I envisioned them as real insects crawling over me with ugly articulated forms. A more terrifying image could not have been conjured up in a child's mind.

"No bugs!" I shrieked. "Take it off me! Let me go! I want my grandma!" I howled again, "I don't want them either! Grandma, help! Don't cover them in! I don't want them in my bed!" But the words fell on the deaf ears of the unattractive nurse. The only answers were the echoes of her horrid footsteps in the deserted hallway. They were echoes that ricocheted across my mind for months as I lay in bed, trapped in the tomb of my little-girl body that would not obey.

The first day I thought the doctors would fix me and that I would only be there overnight. I knew that physicians knew everything about making people better, and surely my mother and father would come in the morning. They would bring my doll named Ochie and my favorite grandmother. And I would sleep at grand-mother's house one night—then they'd take me home and I'd snuggle with Ochie in my own warm bed. I would be strong again, and the bugs that I could not see would be gone forever.

When the sun rose the next day, the dawn of loneliness painted the room in crimson. Hours became days. Days divided to weeks. And weeks metastasized into months. Then the months malignantly grew to nearly a year.

I heard whispered voices outside my room every day. I found it amazing how hearing improves when there is nothing to do but listen. "The poor thing," said the voices that thought I could not notice. "It's too bad she's going to die. She's a cute one! Look at those innocent blue eyes, the blond curls."

"Tsk Tsk. Such a shame," they would repeat, clicking their tongues like hens. They told each other these horrible things in whispery words and hushed voices they thought I could not hear. Some cried softly. Others were cruel and peevish and told supercilious jokes, which they thought I could not understand.

Some faces that stared down on me seemed to sneer in mock pity. Others snickered under their breath at private inside humor that caused outward pain. A few were angels of kindness sent from above. Some came right away when I called. But others left me stinking in my mess for what seemed like hours before they came with their wrinkled noses and covered mouths.

I remember when time mushroomed and boredom grew more cancerous. The tedium grew like a festering boil. As the hands of the clock raced one another, ennui ate the calendar like a ravenous beast.

I refused to believe them when they said I was going to die. I was incarcerated in my immobile body, unable to feed myself and barely able to smile. But I had the greatest gift. It was a gift that the evil of illness and torture of incapacity could not take from me. My mind could wander free, my spirit unfettered by the bonds of earthly immobility. I could still believe. And I wielded the most powerful weapon in the entire universe; I knew that I was a child of the Most Supreme, Most High God. And I could pray to Him. Nothing—not sheets, nor bugs, nor paralysis, nor loneliness, nor boredom— nothing could take that power away from me.

I lay looking at the ceiling hour after hour, day after day, week after week. I wondered at the pattern the cracks made. I tried to make sense of hushed conversations down the hall. I tried to be brave, but when the angel of death walked the halls at night and took some of the others, I was afraid.

As fearful as I was at times, I could not run away. I was, after all, unable to move. I always wondered where my parents were, and I did not understand why they didn't often come to visit. Month slid into month, and I still could not comprehend why I could not get well. I was suspended in a purgatory of childhood chronic illness, neither well enough to sit up by myself nor sick enough to lie down in a coffin.

My mind couldn't grasp the abstract concepts that my parents were poor and had to work every day to even be able to afford the long trip to the hospital. I did not know why they couldn't hug me. I couldn't understand that they were consumed with sadness because they had spent the last of their money to drive 120 miles in a world at war and a nation at ration to see their dying little girl. And that they didn't have extra money for presents.

My parents lived in a one-horse town 120 miles away. They could not see me with any meaningful frequency. In 1941, when cars were slower and gas was rationed, 120 miles was not the same as 120 miles on smooth concrete at 80 miles per hour in air-conditioned comfort. When they did come, they looked down on me with the unreadable expressions of stone deities not empowered to render salvation.

Although they were underprivileged and neither parent had completed high school, my mother and father knew that people died of my disease. They read it in the newspapers and heard it from their friends. I didn't have such luxury of reading: I couldn't pick up a paper even if I could have been able to read it well enough to understand. But I still perceived that others died. They disappeared from the rooms and others took their places.

It was funny how I could tell that the adults thought I was going to die even when they didn't verbalize it. But even with this understanding, I could not fathom why my parents could not be with me every day. Such is the concrete reasoning of a six year old.

My mother and father wouldn't tell me that I would likely die. But I could see it in their eyes. I could tell. I thought maybe that's why they didn't come. Or perhaps they thought they would get my bugs. Thoughts such as these drilled like termites in my mind boring deeper and eating at the very structure that housed hope.

Being a quadriplegic is an interesting thing. One has nothing. No possessions because even if you had them you couldn't lift them. You have no control. You can't brush your teeth, or walk to the bathroom, or even scratch an itch. When it is cold, you can't reach over and pull up the covers. And how do you shiver when you are paralyzed?

All you have is your intellect. But what a gift is a mind! How hot the fire that tempers the soul of one with the privilege of such a trial. Some fires burn hotter for some than others. Some burn at early ages, others in mid-life, and still others as the breath of life is about to return to its Creator.

Paralysis is the cross also borne by Steven Hawking. His body is fettered, but his mind wanders the far reaches of the universe and ponders physics. My little mind wandered and came to rest on the Creator of the universe rather than His creation.

In my little girl's imagination, in my bed of paralysis, some days I could fly. I would float out of bed and down the hall. Effortlessly, I would glide out the door and over the grass. Other boys and girls would look up at me and say, "See that girl, she can fly!" In my mind's eye, I would go home and be able to deftly scoop up my tattered little doll and amaze her with my prowess.

Dreams, wonderful dreams, would come to me at night, but each time I awoke it was the same. White sheets, rails so high that I couldn't see over the top, and my friend the ceiling above—the only thing I could see outside of my bed. The drudgery of each day marched on like a bad movie that would never end.

Doctors were powerless against the monster that I fought. Nurses were both angels and demons. They fed me and changed me and sometimes brushed my hair.

Some couldn't make eye contact, a few had pity, others fear. I remember their faces to this day. They were caricatures that would pop over the rails and stare down on me. Some faces were kind, some were not. A few had pity, some seemed cruel. The gracious ones gave me strength. The believing ones gave me hope. The kind ones gave me serenity. The others gave me nightmares.

Loneliness consumed because I didn't have many visitors, and unlike hospitals today, children then didn't have television or video games. Additionally, I was too weak to hold up a book for most of my incarceration. The rails, too high to see over, went up early in my adventure when I fell out of bed and landed on the floor with all of the grace of a sack of potatoes.

At the times when people did visit, they would ask how I was. I would shout with all the six-year-old strength I could muster, "I'm just fine!" When I said I was fine, I believed. What I believed I became.

Many a day went by with nobody visiting me at all. I was told later that two ladies met every morning and prayed for me. Recalling this, I am sure that on the days when no one visited, the King of Kings was there holding my bedrail, staring into my blue eyes, softly whispering that my faith had already made me whole.

On the days the staff gave me a bath in warm water and the effect of gravity was neutralized, I could move a little. Oh how it felt good to move once again, but as soon as the bath was over, when I was out of the water, I could not move at all.

"Paralyzed" and "infantile paralysis" were the big words the grown-ups used to describe my condition. What horrible words for a six year old to learn! I loathed them. I was not an infant, and I did not want to be called a paralytic. The sound of them, purulent with static, played again and again in my mind like a scratched record. Such were the names of the jailers who held me in the prison of my body.

Polio was epidemic at the time. It was a disease for which there was little understanding and no cure. Tens of thousands were infected, maimed, disabled, and killed by it. It was the forgotten prison of World War II. And the iron lung was the coach upon which many were carried, slowly but assuredly, to their graves.

As bad as I was, not being able to move things below my neck, I knew there were others worse than me. I recall the pity even I, as a little girl, felt for a schoolteacher who was paralyzed from the eyelids to her toes. She could not even move her mouth.

After a time, it became more work to breathe. The hushed discussions of the pretty little blond girl who will die became more frequent. I refused to believe them. Even when it became more difficult to move air in and out of my lungs, I was *not* going to die.

At that point, it seemed the future for me was life in a device they called the iron lung. The doctors made it seem a certainty. "Freedom from the struggle of the diaphragm," they would repeat. Some nurses cried when they heard it. They couldn't hide their emotion from me. I saw their red cheeks and swollen eyes. I knew. But I chose not to believe in the salvation of steel.

I prayed. But I didn't know what to pray for. I knew I didn't want to go in that metal machine. It would eat me with a mouth far more cruel than the sheet that had consumed me at the beginning of my hospitalization.

RESCUED BY THE GREAT-GRANDDAUGHTER OF A HORSE THIEF

In answer to my prayers, a new nurse appeared at my bedside. She talked with a funny accent and was from a faraway land where there was no war and no snow. Such a place seemed mystical to me. In my lifetime, I had never been to a location that never had snow. This country with no blizzards was called Australia. And the nurse was Sister Elizabeth Kenny.

I didn't know why they called her "Sister." Maybe she was someone's sister. But I didn't know whose sister she was. I knew nuns were called sister. But she was supposed to be a nurse, not a nun. Grown-ups sometimes used some funny words. Grown-ups were a strange lot. They said I was going to die too. But I knew I wasn't. I just wasn't.

One morning I woke up and heard arguing outside my room. The air seemed thicker and it was harder to breathe than normal. I was sweating, and as usual, I couldn't pull my sheets back by myself.

As I struggled to inhale, I heard hushed voices call my nemesis by name once again. In my child's lexicon, *death* was a word I could understand. For me, it lurked down the hall like a living creature. Its breath was the hiss of the iron lung. It would stalk the halls stealing children away in the night.

When they wheeled the iron lung into my room and put it next to my bed, I could feel the temperature drop. It was like a block of ice. Sinister and dark as doom, it stood open-mouthed in my room and silently beckoned. The iron lung was the maw of death. I could feel its silent yawn, hungrily waiting to be fed a little girl.

I knew people made wills when they died. I thought of all of my material possessions and wondered who I should give them to. I had a small doll, a little buggy, a little toy iron, and a small wooden horse that my father made. When the iron lung was wheeled in I knew I should have written my will down. Even then, when asked how I was, I would say, "Fine."

I recognized the voices I heard on that day. One was the chief doctor. I didn't know his name, but the other doctors seemed to follow him around like ducks follow their mothers. He was just the big-duck doctor. And he seemed older than the rest. There were also the little-duck doctors, the ones that followed him around, quacking in hushed voices as they trailed. I could hear their littler footsteps following behind their master when they were on the move.

I heard them every day and listened when stopped outside my door. There was no TV to distract me. This was nearly all the entertainment I had.

This day when they stopped outside my door it was different. The doctors' voices were more animated than usual. Something was happening. I felt the air stick like peanut butter in my throat as I listened. It was thick and heavy and hard to get it into my lungs. Could it be the weather? I wondered.

"It's my feeling she must go into the iron lung. Her

breathing is labored and she's starting to sweat," said one of the little-duck doctors in his little-quack voice. He had seen me earlier that morning and noted that something was different.

"I agree," said the big-duck doctor, stepping into the room. "Notice how her ribs protrude each time she breathes. And look at the suprasternal notch. That motion is called 'tugging.' It means she's working harder to breathe. She won't have much time unless we proceed with the therapy you recommend. Very good, Doctor."

"No," argued the lady with the funny accent. "I won't let you."

There was a stunned silence. The little-duck doctors didn't say a word. Someone coughed down the hall. Further on someone dropped a bedpan and it clanged on the floor. The iron lung waited and silently hungered for a scared little girl.

In those days, nurses rose and gave up their seats when doctors entered a room. They scrambled to get coffee for the doctors and hurried to give them the patient's charts. They used phrases like, "Yes, Doctor," and "Right away, sir." They did not argue. They did not say "No." They did not say, "I won't let you."

The older doctor broke the silence. I couldn't see his face, but I imagined a smirk there. He sounded indignant. And set on proving her wrong. Even at my expense. Even if I was eaten by the iron lung and carried in it, like the steel hearse that it was to my grave.

"And you, with your learned experience, you beg to differ, Sister Kenny?" he asked in his grave and gravelly voice.

"Yes, sir," she said. "Putting her in that machine of

yours will kill her," she continued. I felt the tremor in her voice as she spoke.

The little-duck doctors laughed. I heard another nurse clear her throat. The room was still again. I worked to breathe. The machine waited for me in sinister silence.

"And what do you think will cure her? Your hot rags?" said the older doctor, clearing his throat.

There was another quack of a snicker from the little-duck doctors. Feet shuffled on the hard floor. A fly buzzed near the ceiling.

"I do. I think that if we wrap her in hot packs for a prolonged period, she can get better!" the Australian nurse proclaimed.

"Very well," said the older doctor seriously. "Your reputation has preceded you. I've heard something of your hot-pack treatments. But I don't really believe it myself. And you haven't much time. It looks like perhaps tomorrow she'll be sick enough to buy a one-way ticket to the iron lung. We'll leave it next to her for now. I think she'll need it."

"But I'll have to have some help. She'll have to be wrapped in hot packs continuously all night long tonight. We really can't spare much time," said Sister Kenny. "Who can help me?" she pleaded.

No one answered.

"Nurses?" she queried.

"I'm sorry, Sister. We have our medicine rounds. And we have to change the sheets."

"Doctors?" she pleaded.

The silence sang a lonely note in the song of my life in that moment. One voice in the background said, "A nurse thinks she's going to get a doctor to help her. Next thing she'll be operating and we'll be handing her the instruments." It was a little-duck doctor again, quacking his little-duck humor.

There was laughter. Then footsteps pattered quietly down the hall. A face appeared over the bed rail. It was one of the nurses I knew. She didn't look me in the eye. I knew she didn't think the hot rags would work. And she couldn't—or wouldn't—help Sister Kenny on this night. I didn't even know if Sister Kenny was going to come, but I held onto hope. It was the only thing left that I had the strength to grasp.

After the morning rounds that day, my bedside nurse smiled weakly and said, "It's okay, sweetie. They'll put you in the nice iron lung and everything will be all right after that." I didn't believe that anything would be okay in an iron long.

So I talked to the King who came to live among us long ago, who my grandmother had told me about. She said we could ask Him things and He would hear us and answer if it was in His plan. She also said He was still alive even though He had died. As a small child, I didn't really understand how He was alive and yet had died. But I did know one thing: I was *not* going to be eaten by that iron mouth of death.

Later that evening, I heard footsteps approaching my bed. It's funny how you can begin to recognize them if you cannot see the person and how hearing becomes so much more acute when you cannot see (as I could not see over my rails). In this case, I could tell it wasn't someone I knew by the footfalls. I did realize that it was a woman, though. I could recognize the clacking the heels made on the cold hard floor. And she was pushing a cart with squeaky wheels. *Was it someone coming to feed me to the iron mouth?* I wondered.

"It's just you and me, sweetheart," said the nurse with the funny accent. Sister Kenny smiled sweetly as she explained what she was going to do.

The night she began was long and agonizing. The packs felt good at first. Then they were like coals from the depths of hell. I could see the sweat bead on her forehead and strands of hairs stick to her sweaty skin. Sister Kenny wiped back her hair each time she packed me. I could tell she was tired, but she kept up the pace. Her face wasn't pretty to me. But it was earnest. It was the face of my Savior in the form of a woman.

She did it all for a little girl she did not know, in a country far from her home. I do not know to this day how or why she risked her heath, her life, and her reputation by coming to Minnesota. It seems to this day she was simply a paladin sent by God.

God, who knows all and sees all from the end to the beginning, first saved a horse thief in order to save me. Australia is not only unique because of its population of strange marsupials and for its status as the only country that is also a continent. It is also one of a kind because of its history: it was initially largely populated by convicts punished by deportation.

James Moore was transported from Donegal, Ireland, in 1828 after being convicted of stealing a horse. I'm certain that he would have been proud to know his great-granddaughter, the instrument of my temporal salvation, Elizabeth Kenny.

Unwavering in her dedication, this great-granddaughter of a horse thief packed me in hot packs all night at least once. In that era—to pack someone in hot-packs all night was back breaking work. There were no microwaves. No safe electric pads. There were only hot rags cut from surplus wool blankets. The hot rags had to be wrung out by a roller on an old-fashioned washing machine, one after another after another.

I was regularly packed by Sister Kenny's protocol for almost a year. All the while, the iron lung waited expectantly for a meal of a little girl basted in hot packs if the therapy should not succeed. I knew some doctors didn't think it would work and some even expected her to fail. The words of a child return to me when I think of this trying time. I wrote them down once: "An iron lung was brought in next to me. The doctors wanted to put me in now. Sister Kenny came to my rescue and stayed all night with me during the crisis, not letting the doctors put me in the iron lung. She said, 'People don't live long in the iron lung. It is a machine that breathes for you. Once put in, patients must stay in. All they can see is the ceiling.'"

The hours of that pivotal night with Sister Kenny wore on. But still she packed me in the artificial warmth of the hot rags. I dozed on and off as little girls do, but Sister Kenny didn't sleep at all. The towels were wrapped around my neck like the jewelry of the tribeswomen I had seen in National Geographic who stretched their necks. I could feel my neck extend. The fears from sublime to ridiculous chewed on my consciousness like rats on a corpse. How could they pack me in hot packs if I were in the iron lung? What if my neck started to stretch and didn't go back to normal? I could feel it lengthen already. My fears grew—what if I had such a tall neck I had to bend over to walk through doorways? I would be Giraffe Girl!

I also knew if my neck stretched out, the ghastly goslings of medicine would return and not leave me alone. The lines of big-duck doctors and the little quacks that followed them would never stop.

I recall how at first I could not move any limb at all. I could hardly swallow. Slowly, painfully, after months of nurses moving my arms for me I could do a little on my own. The hot-pack therapy lasted for nearly a year. Every fifteen minutes a new hot, moist, wool rag was wrung out between the rollers of an old washing machine and placed on me. It went on for twenty-four hours per day, seven days per week.

In addition to my difficulty moving, there were times when I found I couldn't speak. I remember once when I couldn't speak for five whole days. When I could miraculously speak again, my first words were "chocolate cake." To this day, chocolate cake remains one of my favorite foods.

One day, late in the course of my hospitalization, when I could move a little again, I became a six-year-old semi-paralyzed vandal. On this day, the nurses said I could go visit other patients in rooms in the late afternoon if I did not have a temperature. I was so excited waiting for the time to pass. It was to be my first time out of the bed.

Hours passed like snails racing caterpillars. When my temperature was finally taken, it soared and I was informed I could not go. After being told I couldn't go visiting, I was in a very cross mood indeed. To register my unhappiness I made a tiny hole in my sheet with a little pair of scissors I had. I then inserted my toe in it and ripped it into a bigger one. I was mad as a wet cat, but later I was sorry for my effrontery. But that was the limit of my cheekiness and all the retaliation I could muster for the unfairness of the situation. To this day I am sad about how I ruined that sheet. I never did it again.

After nearly a year of hot-pack therapy, I regained the strength to walk. Luckily I didn't have to hunker down when I passed from one room to another like the giraffe I imagined they would make me.

Finally, after nearly a year in the hospital, I was healed and they let me out. Hospital personnel offered me a wheelchair and tried to insist I use it. But I would *not* accept a ride; I had to toddle out by myself. I still have the memory of walking down the stairs on the way out of the building where I was kept hostage for a year. The steps I took were slow and unsteady, and I had to hold onto the rail as if it were my Savior's staff.

As I gingerly walked out of the hospital and stared down at my feet on the ground, I couldn't believe they were mine. Was this, I wonder, what the lame man felt after the miraculous healing by Jesus? Did he stare down at his sandals with the realization that every solitary step was a miracle of its own merit?

BREAKFAST WITH MY SAVIOR

As a reward for the temerity of Sister Kenny and as a testimony to the God who knows when sparrows fall and who heals small children when He wills, I was not put in the iron lung that was wheeled into my room. Instead, after I was saved, I was invited to breakfast with the famous nurse who fought with doctors on my behalf and stayed up all night with me on at least one occasion.

That special breakfast was the highlight of my little life to that point and one of the most memorable ever to this very moment. I had never been taken out to breakfast before and rarely ever since. Even though it was a real treat for a girl so poor to be taken out at all, the special treat was eating breakfast with my knight in shining armor—the one who had rescued me from the depths of the dungeon of infantile paralysis in the evil castle of polio.

I do not remember exactly what we ate on the morning I dined with my liberator or where we ate it. But I am certain of one thing: there was another Savior with us that day at the table. The One who saved us both was there, unseen, smiling with us, and reveling in our joy

At this point in my life as I look back, that was a small taste of what it will be like when we sit down for a meal with Jesus in heaven when we are redeemed. The food will no doubt be marvelous—not like the pitiful meals we poor folk share here below. We will dine on the fruit of the Tree of Life! But the real reward will not be eating out or the taste of the food. It will be sitting with our Savior, the Prince of Peace, His Majesty, the King of Kings.

Words cannot explain my adoration on that morning. I was a little girl, a poor youngster, who on good years got an orange for Christmas, sitting with this famous nurse who came all the way from a magical place across the prairie and over the sea called Australia. The same nurse who stood up to the big-duck doctor and argued with him and stayed up all night with me and packed me in hot packs. And, this hero was taking me, *me,* to breakfast! I was somebody!

I can't wait to have breakfast with her again someday in the Kingdom. We'll both raise our glasses to the One who came over the prairie, from across the ocean and across the very universe to save both of us. We will toast the One who volunteered to come across space and time to our tiny speck of a world. The One who left the presence of the Most High God and who stood up to the big duck Satan and said, "No, you're not taking these children to the pit! I'm staying up with them! I'm going to that cross for them. And I'm going to take them to breakfast with me someday when they are whole!"

THE RED WAGON OF PLENTY

I was excited beyond expression to be home after my release from the hospital. After all, I had been away for almost a year. My possessions were few—but my favorite remained my doll, Ochie. We were a poor family. Today, one might describe such a state as being economically disadvantaged. I didn't understand poverty then. When you were poor, you were regular. We were regular. Everyone else was rich.

When I think about my recovery and my return home, my mind wanders to my father. He was a pillar of strength, a paragon of values, and perhaps, the one who spawned creativity in my own children, which in turn led to our unique ministry at Noah's Ark.

Henry Richard Braley, my dear old dad, was the oldest of eight children. Unlike my mother, who was born in a farmhouse, he was born in the city. The family told stories from the time before I was born about how he had a job as a small child to help support his seven brothers and sisters. As I write this, my mind wanders to my aunt, Della Hofstrand, his sole remaining sister. She has fond memories of my father's golden heart and willingness to sacrifice for his family from the time he was small.

My father loved airplanes, tinkering with inventions, and riding motorcycles. Some of my own earliest memories rode on two wheels. I have fond memories of my father's first motorcycle. In the depression era, he used to ride five of us on it at once. The smallest in our group rode on the gas tank; I rode behind my dad, and behind me my grandmother, with my mother acting the role of the caboose in the very back. Those were the days!

Before I was born, my paternal grandfather was "unavailable," so by the time my dad finished the eighth grade, he had to quit school to work and help support the family. Being a child and having limited means, he used his little red wagon to help make a living for them. He worked hard and made daily deliveries in the neighborhood instead of studying or playing with his friends. His allegiance to family remained unwavering through the rest of his life.

I always admired my father. He was a good God-fearing man who worked hard and wore a clean smile, no matter how soiled his clothes were from the labor he endured. My dad was a man with a mischievous glint in his eye, a quick snapping-turtle smile, and wit as sharp as a razor. He was the one in the room who always had a new joke to tell which would make a crowd roar. If you asked him what he did, he would probably tell you that he was a "tinkerer."

I can envision him as a middle-aged man in his shop, smiling and wallowing in the company of his homemade tools. Electric motors mounted on wood platforms turned belts that ran saws, sanders, gizmos, and gadgets little understood by people not endowed with his guts. I remember how he sipped a soft drink when taking a break in his shop and how the slurping sound added to the cacophony of the noisy machines. And I recall the smell of sawdust and how it peppered the air each time he cooked up a new creation.

In my mind's eye, I can still see his gray-white curly hair on end. He sometimes looked like a professor in an early electricity lab who used too much voltage. There were deep laugh lines etched in his face, baked there as if marks in sun-kissed clay. To me it was obvious: the master sculptor chiseled them there through years of satisfaction with his creations.

He would eagerly grasp new ideas and enlarge them with a wave of his hand, marinate them with his smile, and spice them with the sparkle in his bright blue eyes. My mother was there too, not far from his shop, "Hank," she would say, "Put on this apron to protect your clothes. You're always a messin' them." I never saw anyone so usefully messy in my life.

Although he listed his profession as a printer and called himself a tinkerer, some would refer to him as an inventor. He may have been an inventor—but he was definitely one who never wanted any credit. When I look back in time, I sometimes consider his many inventions. One of my favorites remains the fantastic futuristic ice boat he made in the late 1920s or early 1930s. With a Model T engine, a hand-carved propeller, some railroad parts, and a frame with a homemade sleek aerodynamic cowl, he created a boat that would fly across the frozen lakes of Minnesota. It flew driven not only by an engine from the factory of Henry Ford, but by the elbow grease and power of the ingenuity of Henry Braley.

The tinkerer was the first on his block to have an electric garage door opener. I think it was in the 1950s, and of course, he built it himself with plans of his own design. He was a humble man who didn't want fame or fortune—so he refused to apply for patents or market his inventions.

I also recall how no problem was too small for my father's attention. When his grandson, Happy—my second son—was little, he caught a frog and wondered how he would feed it. My dad created a fly trap with a funnel of screen and a box. The frog was well fed. And when Happy wanted to catch a live mouse to see it, my father whipped up a trap to catch one. He loved children and would gleefully entertain them for hours by such feats as whittling a propeller or crafting a tiny flying machine with miscellaneous parts such as a spool of thread and a straw.

My father was fascinated by more things than I can list, but among them was the miracle of flight. At one time, he owned a half interest in an airplane with another man. But as human nature would have it, when his partner would fly, fuel would disappear, oil wouldn't be added, and the airplane partnership ultimately dissolved, to the unfettered joy of my mother.

When he married, he married an educated woman, by his standards. My mother finished the ninth grade before having to quit and work on the farm her family owned. Her work ethic paralleled that of my father. But she outdid him in school by one year of education.

I often wonder what heights my father would have reached had he the opportunity to have more than an eighth-grade education. His cleverness seemed without boundaries. Those who remember him always recall his inventions and unusual ideas.

When I was a late teen, my father bought an empty tract of land with a partner and together they made a row of cottages by hand and sold them. By a flip of a coin, the street was named after us and the project became "Braley Avenue." The cottages were small, two-bedroom units built on tiny pilasters. I went by a few years ago to see if they were still there. As a testament to my father's craftsmanship, they were still standing. My husband and I rented one of them in our big spending days when we were first married.

My maternal grandparents had talent that perhaps also washed downstream in the river of genes to my own offspring and that was also helpful in the creation of our ministry. My mother's father was a fiddler and her mother an organist. They played so well and so frequently that her friends would often ask her how the party was. She'd answer by asking, "What party?" They'd respond, "You know, the one at your house with all the fiddling and organ music last night!"

My mother wanted to be a schoolteacher. But this plan was at odds with her family's need for help on the farm. She solved the problem when she found a benefactor who was willing to pay for her schooling. When he died, it was—tearfully—back to work on the farm for her. She was always sad about that and always wondered what her life would have been like had she been a schoolteacher. I loved her just fine with the education level that she attained.

Life is strange like that. Sometimes the forces of God wash out the path we are traveling on the roadway of life and push us into unanticipated adventures. On occasion we slide down the mountain when the path is completely eroded and land on a different trail altogether. It is all in the Master's plan.

On some byways, we encounter slippery rocks; on others, we run into stinging nettles. We will all find wolves that stalk us from the forest on life's path and vultures that silently menace overhead. Those of us who look will find good friends to travel with. In my own life, there have been wolves, vultures, and avalanches. By the grace of our Creator, I have been able to keep on my path and have also been blessed with good family and friends with which to travel.

In my own life's path, the wolves of polio glared at me with their menacing yellow eyes for an entire year. The following year, the lion of leukemia roared, and still further on came the avalanche of an alcoholic.

I always remember that in order to climb a higher mountain in my life, I must first descend off of the peak where I stand. I know that if I don't, I can never climb to a higher summit.

We all need to walk our own trail in life and travel at our own pace. That is certain. We must also face our own obstacles. So stare down your wolves, find good friends to walk with, have faith in God, keep moving on your own pathway, and reach your own zenith!

THE JOURNEY WEST AND ANOTHER DEATH SENTENCE

During World War II, after the battle of polio and before the skirmish of leukemia, the local economy wasn't good for a printer. After my father lost his job, my parents begged ration cards from friends and family, loaded all of the worldly possessions we could fit into our car, and headed west. The things we couldn't stuff into the vehicle we tied to the top and to the front and rear bumpers. Do you remember the opening scene in the old sitcom, The Beverly Hillbillies? That automobile was much nicer and loaded with fewer items than ours!

When I was a little girl, my father worked in a print shop. He had worked there since he was an adolescent. He worked eight hours per day, but when the economy got bad, he would check out and work another four hours without pay. He tried almost everything to keep his job. But eventually all was in vain because his employment evaporated like Minnesota snow in the spring. The war needed ships, ships needed welders, and my father needed a job. So we migrated west, to the land of shipyards. It was a promised land that did not flow with milk and honey, but rather with steel and solder.

Upon loading our car to the fenders, my parents found there was nowhere for me to sit. Ultimately I perched on top of the bundles of some of our meager possessions and we were off. Minnesota snow was eagerly traded for Washington rain. During the course of our epic journey west, we experienced flat tires and even a blizzard, but nothing deterred us from our goal. My father kept driving, and I proudly sat high up on a throne of our belongings, watching the world go by.

Ultimately, after many days of travel in a very old and rickety car loaded to the gills, we made it to the west coast. When we arrived in Camas, Washington, we were fortunate to stay with relatives until we were able to move to our very own shack.

The tiny hut into which we moved wasn't really fit for human habitation. One night, shortly after we arrived, my mother awoke to check on me. She was shocked to see a huge rat sitting on my head peering up at her with its beady little eyes. It seemed ready to make a meal of her precious daughter.

That was enough for her—she told my dad we were leaving, and we had to move at once. My mother didn't like the scaly-tailed things much from the time she was a little girl. She had a previous run in with a rat, which I think gave her a special disdain for the creatures.

As I mentioned previously, my mother lived on a farm when she was a child. Like most kids who live on farms, she had chores. Chief among her many responsibilities was to fetch the water from the well for the family. Their well was the old-fashioned type, and one had to use a bucket and a rope to draw the water.

One day after her chores, she took a drink from the well, but on this particular day she thought that the water tasted horrible. I think children have better taste buds than adults. It's probably why they can be picky eaters. The bad flavor she found was subtle and one that she could detect but her parents could not. It wasn't strong enough to be identified. Her parents couldn't taste any difference in the water, so they told her what most parents would: "Don't be silly, the water's fine."

But she wouldn't be dissuaded. She thought the water was awful and wouldn't drink it. Eventually she walked all the way to the neighbors' house (not a small feat for a little girl with a big bucket) to get her own water. Her parents insisted on their own well water, to their detriment.

That is also the way life works. Warnings of badness in life come from small voices. These small warnings earnestly urge us to avoid the taste of evil and to keep ourselves pure. And sometimes evil begins so subtly it is difficult to tell when it takes hold in our lives if we are not careful. There are times in our lives when we must listen to the warnings of others and heed them.

Eventually the water got worse and the family found the source of her concern: A dead rat was floating in the well!

Many years after her rat-in-the-well, and after my own rat-on-the-head adventure in the shack, we moved to my uncle's prune orchard in Vancouver, Washington. In the orchard, we had the double benefit of picking fruit and having a place that did not come with beady-eyed, scaly tailed pets.

My parents managed to acquire an eight by twenty-four foot trailer, and our little family made our home in it at the orchard. Life in a corner of Uncle Charlie's plot was not easy. And as you can imagine, it was hard to keep clean living in such an environment.

Running water was scarce, but sharing was not. So we took turns taking a bath on Saturday night whether we needed it or not. As the trailer didn't have a proper bathtub, we bathed in a folding washtub in the living room. I was a little girl and always the cleanest, so I got to go first. After my mother, my father had his turn. I'm glad I didn't have to look at the water after he got out!

We made do with what we had. We did not accept any public assistance, and we worked hard. We survived on staples of rice and beans, fruit and vegetables, a little meat when we had it, but mostly we thrived on a diet of hard work.

Hard work is the nutrient most lacking in the metaphorical diet of many residents of the United States. We were extremely poor but found a way to get by without aid from the government. I do not wish to throw rocks at anyone receiving such help, but I see problems with accepting it long term.

The problem as I see it with public assistance is that it attenuates one's drive to work hard and succeed. Let's look at an example of an individual who sprains an ankle. If the treatment is an electric wheelchair for—forever—instead of crutches and progressive walking, what happens to that person's ability to walk? If a person doesn't walk for years, what happens to his or her leg muscles?

When we were down, we pulled ourselves up. When our ankles were sprained, we strapped on a splint we made ourselves and we used crutches *only* until we could walk again under our own power. That was the spirit that led us to do the ministry. We did it with the help of God, family, friends, and our own ingenuity rather than sitting back until someone did it for us and handed us the keys.

And if I can digress about the depression for a moment, I must add we saved most everything, and learned to fix everything that couldn't be saved as it was. This day and age, everything is disposable. Devices made in China or Korea are so cheap to construct, repair is now impractical. They must be thrown out, not fixed. As a result, children do not learn age-old techniques of problem solving. I worry about this. What happens in society when children learn to throw out and buy new rather than to solve? What happens when education becomes simply rote regurgitation of data and is not solution oriented?

Shortly after moving into the trailer in the prune orchard, my father started work in the shipyard, and my mother was soon to follow. Finally, they had jobs and we had a little bit of money again. Satan often picks these times in life, when you are just getting ahead again, to attack.

Like a sin that starts small, the lump on my finger began as a tiny little blemish. Later that day, it grew, and in a short time, a red streak began to snake its way up my arm. They admitted me to the hospital that night, and the doctor felt I wouldn't have lived to see the dawn if they hadn't brought me when they did.

Sharp words about death pointed in your direction are always scary. They are especially hard to hear as a seven year old, even if you have heard them before. But

I had heard them before and would hear them again. While waiting to be seen by the doctor for an infected arm, I remember sitting on my dad's lap reading the funny papers. He tried so hard to comfort me.

That was when my nose started to bleed. It wasn't a drip or a drop—blood ran out of me like a faucet. It went on my chest, my hands, the paper, and all over my father. It was not only horrible—it was leukemia!

Although the road to Washington was free of mishaps greater than a flat tire and a blizzard, at the age of seven, the lion of leukemia roared at me from the sidelines of my pathway in life. It growled as frighteningly as polio did a year before and locked me in the hospital for nearly another year of my young life. Once again in its shadow, the skeletal hooded form of death lurked.

Death wears many clothes, uses many hats, and drives an assortment of vehicles. For some, as for my youngest brother, Gaylen, who was also called Gaylord, it came as a left turn in a pickup truck piloted by a man with a co-pilot named Alcohol. For his second wife, it came in a boat with a biting propeller, and for my nephew, a faulty chain holding logs on a truck.

But sometimes with the help of our guardian angels, death swings hard with his scythe and narrowly misses. You can almost feel the air as the blade whirrs by your head on these occasions. It's the time when the hand of your invisible guardian holds and protects you. You have no doubt had these in your own life and know what I mean.

When death narrowly missed me by means of both leukemia and polio, I can't help to think that my guardian angel was there with unseen hands, pushing the scythe away and telling the specter of death it was not yet my time. There was work for me yet to do.

Schoolmates passed me another year, and the details of my illness remain fuzzy. I do not know what kind of leukemia I had. But as my gums grew down over my teeth, I have been told in retrospect that it was a form that medicine calls "hairy cell leukemia."

I recall little about that time except that once again I was not expected to live. This time name of the jailor who kept me captive was not polio. It was leukemia. And the bonds that held me were infections and bleeding rather than paralysis.

I remember the blood, and I recall the infections. But what I missed most was not being able to run or play. Once again, long hours of boredom tormented me and I made up my mind that I was not going to die.

I remember going back to school when I recovered. The noise of playing children was deafening. When I was locked up in the hospital, I couldn't hear my play-mates' laughter outside where I longed to be. In the children's ward, all of the kids were quiet and did not scream and shout with the joy of life.

When death tried again that year, my guardian angel worked overtime. Appendicitis fell like an uprooted tree upon my life's path, as if the roaring of the figurative lion of leukemia wasn't enough.

I was lying in the hospital with leukemia when the abdominal pain came. Death scurried like a crab down the corridor and seemed to hide in my room once more. Again, as I was incarcerated in a teaching facility, I was cared for by a flock of big-duck doctors and little-duck doctors in training. They stopped outside doors and discussed lofty matters of life and death in hushed tones each morning.

At age seven, I was able to recall details better. I remember one conversation quite well. There were two surgeons arguing outside my room. The discussion was about me and my old nemesis, my hooded enemy, Death. It was almost as if he were a creature who had trailed me from Minnesota and loitered again in the shadows. This time death didn't breathe with the susurration of the iron lung. He silently waited for leukemia to do the job that polio wasn't allowed to complete. As that wasn't fast enough to satisfy him, my appendix became inflamed and threatened to explode.

The doctors came into my room and examined me. I am certain my guardian angel was there that day, holding back an act of fate that might have resulted in the world never seeing the ministry of Noah's Ark.

"How are you today?" asked one of the doctors.

"I'm fine," I responded. I'm still "fine" whenever a doctor asks me this question. I'm afraid not to be. After they examined me; the flock of doctors made their way outside where they thought I could not hear. I listened closely and hung on every word. And I remember them clearly to this day:

One doctor said, "I don't think we should operate. She'll die of leukemia anyway. She's almost there now."

I strained harder to hear the response. My heart pounded in my chest. I knew that life hung in the balance. I did not know that if they did not operate, I would likely die a miserable death of peritonitis and pain. If they did, as one doctor noted, I'd probably succumb to leukemia anyway. Either option was bad. In any case, the unseen guy in the black robe carrying a scythe was deprived of the prize of a frightened, lonely little girl once again. But he couldn't have me. Jesus already did. And He had a plan for me that I couldn't have known at that time.

After a theatrical pause, the other doctor countered him and solemnly said, "I think we should operate." At this I smiled, unseen, around the corner. I am sure to this day that my guardian angel whispered in the ear of the man arguing on my behalf. I can't wait to thank him someday.

"Why?" incredulously queried the first doctor "She's going to die anyway. Resources are scarce. There's a war on!"

"Yes," continued the second surgeon. "But we might give her a few months. Maybe she'll even have a few good months."

Listening from the prison of my bed, I decided that I'd be happy with a few good months. After all, I wasn't eaten by the iron lung last year. Who knows what can happen in a few good months?

I can still envision my guardian angel there whispering in the ear of the surgeon who argued for me. I can almost see him poking the doctor in the rib for extra measure. There was another there too; I'm sure a serpent was there, also unseen, bending the ear of the other.

The difference was this, of course: my guardian angel was under the direction of Michael the Archangel, the Prince of Peace, who knows the end from the beginning and the number of hairs on my head. That same

King, who came to save us all, knew what future lay in store for a ministry far removed from that era.

In 1942, the serpent couldn't know about the ministry in the future, but, the Prince of Peace did. The King of Kings knows too about the ministry my grandchildren's children will provide—and the one your children and grandchildren will participate in as well—which none of us can even imagine now in the year 2010.

The motion of the second surgeon was carried, and the operation undertaken instead of me being sent to the undertaker. And I did have a few good months, and a few more, better months. And I'm still having them.

Medical science calls miracles of healing "spontaneous remission." That's what they say I had after the end of that year of sickness. Another year of my life spent in the confines of the hospital.

I was lucky I suppose. What was part of a childhood in a hospital compared to Job's suffering or Moses tending sheep for forty years? It could have been worse.

When I was hospitalized with leukemia there were no Australian nurses with washing machines of warm water and wool hot packs. Instead, there was a good surgeon who, under the influence of the Great Healer, argued on my behalf and won. But I recovered again and the doctors were astounded once more. When I was wheeled out of the institution, I was a thin, pale, skeleton of a girl, who was by this time was developing a strong dislike of hospitals.

ALTAR CALL ON A ROAD TRIP

After I had survived that year and skipped first grade, I was excited to be eight. I didn't know if I'd even live that long, so the birthday was especially sweet. The highlight of my year was another visit to my grandmother in magical Minneapolis. After moving west to Washington, this trip was considerably longer than the 120 miles from Todd County. I rode the bus without an adult along. In those days such travel was common: the bus company would have employees who looked after children on the stops and would herd them back onto the bus after breaks and guide them through transfers.

Although she was a diminutive woman who stood less than five feet tall, my grandmother's faith made her a giant. I'm sure that her prayers were instrumental in saving me from polio, leukemia and appendicitis to that point in my life. On that holiday, she took me to an old fashioned church meeting where there was an altar call.

I had heard about Jesus and experienced answered prayers myself, but I had never officially accepted Him into my heart. When the altar call came at a camp meeting at the Baptist church she attended, I felt my pulse quicken and I started to sweat. I wanted to accept my Savior into my heart. After all, I already knew what it was like to have prayers answered and to be saved. I was excited but shy. First I ran to the front of the church then retreated back to my grandmother. She told me not to be afraid and to march right back up there.

I did go back to the altar, and with the help of my grandmother's prayer, I was not afraid. At the altar they taught me how to pray once more, and I accepted Jesus into my heart on that very day. I find it amazing how Jesus answers prayers even before you ask Him into your heart. What prayers in your life have been answered in your life before you knew Him or accepted Him as your personal Savior?

MOLDY APPLES AND SKELETONS

By the time I had returned to the classroom, memories of long months in health-care facilities were fading and my appendix scar had healed. I was well on my way to lady hood, and my family was doing a little better financially thanks to the cleverness of my eighth-grade educated father. My battles were over for a time, and even World War II had come to a close. The world was again a peaceful place.

Following my string of hospitalizations and brushes with death, I was delighted to be able to attend school. I recall some kind of test and a placement into the grade ahead. How I did well on that exam, I don't know, but it was good enough to be promoted to the second grade. I had to give extra effort in school just to keep up. After all, I had missed almost two years of it while in the hospital in Minnesota with polio and Washington with leukemia. But I managed.

The noise level of children playing was raucous. I had been around children a fair amount as a small child, but they were all in the hospital. Hospitalized children didn't shout and scream. They moan and lay still in their beds. I thought all children were as quiet as the hospitalized type!

We all have experiences with the potential to change our lives. What we do with these experiences is dependent on what meaning we assign to them. Something happened to me in elementary school that I feel changed my life and influenced my ability to create the ministry of Noah's Ark. It was very simple and involved a moldy apple.

When I went back to school, I found that the classroom was like new. It took a while to get the idea of what was required of a student again. At the school I attended, we had desks that had hidden compartments that were accessed by opening the top. They were the storage spaces for books and assignments. I tried my best to get the hang of it again, but it wasn't without the occasional difficulty.

Once I was asked by my teacher to open my desk to retrieve something while she stood by. I opened it in her presence, but inside, I found a moldy apple, crumpled papers, and a broken pencil. I was so embarrassed by these things, I vowed that I would always be prepared and that there would be no moldy apples in my desk from then on. I have found that if one cleans the moldy apples out of one's desk as a child and keeps them out, one doesn't worry about skeletons in the closet as an adult!

THE GILDED GIGGLER

I think personalities are formed before a baby escapes from the womb. Recent medical research seems to indicate that the mental state of the woman during pregnancy actually does influence the personality of the child. My youngest brother was born when I was twelve years old, almost a teen, during a happy point in my mother's life. He had a golden heart and hair to match. He would laugh and giggle at the slightest provocation and hardly ever cried.

He was named Gaylen and everyone called him Gay for short. That was of course many years before the word had a sexual-orientation connotation. In those days, the definition of *gay* was "happy"—and happy he was!

My mother was older when my brother Gaylen was born, so she enjoyed all the help that an adolescent daughter could offer with her new baby. And I loved helping with such a wonderful child. The lessons I learned while taking care of my brother catapulted me ahead in life. My love of children was instrumental in the development of the Noah's Ark theme for our ministry.

When I took care of Gay after school hours, I loved to take him with me everywhere I went. The way he would interact with people was a joy to watch! And I was never so content as when strangers thought that he was mine. He was so wonderful that I wanted to get married so I could have one just like him!

LOCKED IN A CLOSET BY A DRUNK

When I was a teen, girls were groomed to get married and have families rather than pursue careers. I too was raised with this mentality. After taking care of my beloved new baby brother I could indeed envision having a family of my own. As an adolescent, I became more attracted to boys and they more enamored with me. By my late teens, the boys became as drawn to me as bees are to flowers. Of course, I also learned that, like bees, boys can sting.

There was one dating experience that introduced me to the Christian denomination of Seventh-Day Adventism. Considering it in retrospect, it's hard to imagine why I ever gave it a second look later in my life. The experience was not a good one.

When I was a teenager at an all-girls' school, I met a Seventh-Day Adventist boy. He wanted to date me, but I wasn't so sure it was a good idea. I had grown up going to church on Sunday, and he was different than most of the other boys I had known. The difference wasn't so much about the day he worshiped; it was what he did with his time out of school and church.

After I got to know him I thought that *all* Adventists drank and smoked. It is lucky for me that I didn't develop an antipathy to Adventism. Fortunately, the ambassador for Adventism didn't speak for all of his denomination and I later learned that they all didn't smoke and drink. I was astounded to learn later that the denomination is known not only for worshiping on the seventh day Sabbath like the early Christians did, but that it is also known for its health message.

When considering a family, as with everything I did, I wanted to plan ahead. The moldy apple in my drawer that was discovered by my teacher taught me that. Considering such preparation, I thought seriously about where I had lived and where I wanted to reside in the future.

After my childhood in the frigid winters of Minnesota and dreary rain of the Pacific Northwest, I was ready for some sunshine. I had heard about the wondrous land of the sun at the end of the rainbow, called San Diego. And once I went there on a vacation, I always wanted to live there. It was a fantasy land where it was nearly always summer, never snowed, and almost never rained. For a girl growing up knowing hospitals, snow, and rain, it was paradise. After I visited the land of sun with my family, I never got it out of my system.

At the conclusion of my first visit to southern California, I became hooked by the idea that I could move there and raise my children without worry of freezing to death by walking to the mailbox in the wrong clothes or drowning in the rain on the way to school. So, like the vow to remove rotten fruit from my desk and keep it out, I took an oath to myself I would move to San Diego. And I kept my promise.

When a military man proposed to me and offered to

take me back to San Diego, it seemed too good to be true. I learned later that when something seems too good to be true, it often is. We were married in a simple ceremony a short time later in Oregon, then off to San Diego we went.

San Diego was as wonderful as I had remembered it on my first visit. The early fifties was a time when the beauty of the city was in full bloom but it had not yet been discovered by millions. The weather was fantastic, the beaches were delightful, but marriage was awful.

Sometimes a couple doesn't have adequate time to get to know each other before taking a trip down the aisle. In my first marriage, this was the rule, not the exception. In fact, it was the poster marriage for the advertisement of a really long courtship, personality tests, and a lie detector exam. After moving to San Diego, I soon found that my new husband had vices he had kept in the closet when we were dating.

Sharing this portion of my story is most painful. I have suffered oppression in the past, including punishment by parents and the threat of the iron lung. But spousal abuse is something that we often keep hidden and locked away from others. I never wanted to tell anyone about it. I especially didn't want my boys to ever learn about it. But it is a part of my life. As a tongue of the fire that tempered my soul, it helped to give me the strength to create the ministry at Noah's Ark, so I must share it, as agonizing as it was.

My first husband was a boy who wore man's clothes. Like the Adventist youth I dated when I was a teen, I found that he was a drinker. Worse even than the drinking, he smoked like a chimney and hid it from me when we were dating. When I registered my feelings about these irritating habits, his answer was to blow smoke into my face and laugh. That wasn't the answer I was looking for.

He thought it was funny to inhale from his cigarette and blow smoke at me. He would sometimes even blow it right into my mouth. And then he would breathe on me with his alcohol breath. Worse still, he found it hilarious to lock me in a closet at his whim and threaten to beat me.

After three months of this treatment, I called my mother for advice. She told me to stick it out. So I stuck it out for another week before I had had enough. Sometimes we get bad advice in life. Another thing I learned at that time was to identify bad advice when I first hear it.

These lessons were instrumental in guiding my life and development of our ministry at Noah's Ark. We are all human. None of us are immune from the disease of making bad decisions. Wisdom comes from learning from them.

I decided that I had had enough guidance from my mother on the matter and left him without further recommendations from others. I only returned to retrieve the remainder of my possessions. I took a bus home to Oregon right away, with the kind help of the minister of the local Church of God where I attended. Often in life one knows the right thing to do, one just needs to do it. One should also learn to ignore bad advice as soon as it is identified. If you listen to your heart and are open to the voice of the Holy Spirit, you will find that you know what is right.

Those who know me well, including my family, friends, and employees, know that I accept few excuses for not telling the truth. When someone lies, as with my first husband who lied about drinking and smoking, I do not believe them about anything. I also find that smoking and drinking to excess are markers for persons who will likely lie and cheat in the future.

I found that being locked in a closet by a drunk and abusive husband is a lot like lying in a hospital bed paralyzed. You don't have a lot of control. I came out of the closet, regained control, and left. That was something I couldn't do when I had polio or leukemia. A person must also identify what he or she has control over in life. Don't wallow in badness if you can do something about it. If you need a change—make it!

The Blanket of Love

In 1954 I found myself recently divorced from my alcohol abusing first husband and working at Newberry's department store in Portland, Oregon. I was a single girl once again, and the last thing I wanted to think about was being married to the alcohol and nicotine abusing fool. Although I wasn't interested in chasing men, I wasn't opposed to meeting them either. To keep myself busy and get on my feet again I focused on my job and put gentlemen on hold for a while.

Things were looking up for me once more, but as much as I tried to put my bad marriage behind me, it followed in a humorous manner. As I helped customers at Newberry's where I worked, I began to receive wonderful accolades about the beautiful picture of me in the window of a photography studio down the street. I couldn't figure out what they were talking about, so I took it upon myself to take a walk and find out.

As I approached the window, I gasped. As a testament to the skill of the photographer, the studio had blown up a full-sized poster of me in the window of the shop. It was certainly a good representation of what could be produced if they were hired to take pictures. I was a pretty girl, and the picture was well done. The only problem was that I was in my wedding dress, and it was not the image I wanted to project to the world as a single girl!

Meanwhile, my parents moved and were starting to build the houses on Braley Avenue in Coos Bay, Oregon. Family support being paramount, I followed my parents' move and relocated with them to the coast. Having had it with men for the time being, I decided to continue to focus on working and ultimately got a job at Penny's of Coos Bay. It was perhaps the second time in my life when I worked for someone else.

While working at Newberry's and Penny's, I learned lessons about being on time, doing the bidding of my boss, and presenting a good image to the public. It is these simple things that make a good employee great and that philosophy that makes a great business or ministry wonderful. Unfortunately, people sometimes forget about these simple aspects of being a good worker.

One day when I was working as a salesgirl at Penny's, a young man came to buy a blanket. In spite of my bad experience with men so far, this guy seemed special. He was physically fit; he *really* didn't smoke or drink and had a wonderful twinkle in his eye. He left with the blanket and a little piece of my heart that day. Later, we began to see each other and, in a short time, to date more seriously.

I recall one of our first dates. We went together to my annual company picnic, and while we were there, I learned something else about managers: they do not like to lose.

Our company get-together was always like the Norman Rockwell depiction of a small-town, old-fashioned company picnic. In the era before TV-related deconditioning, video game-related muscular atrophy, and ever increasing abdominal girth, people actually ran races and had friendly competitions at such events.

Usually at this affair, the boss won virtually all of the games. He was the sort who was used to having his way and to coming out on top. My date, Irvin, ended his winning streak, and it became quite clear that my supervisor did not like it!

In retrospect, I think that as bad as it was to bring a date that showed up my boss to the company picnic, Irvin's competitiveness was one of the things that initially attracted me to him. He was quiet and humble like my father, and I found out later, he could fix most anything. His skill of being able to make do and repair things catapulted us ahead in life and made our ministry at Noah's Ark possible. For better or worse, I am still in love with him.

SAVED FROM STRANGLING BY A PRAYER

I married Irvin Emery Thrush on December 10, 1955 in a lovely ceremony in North Bend, Oregon. North Bend is a quaint community near Coos Bay. It was, finally, a dream come true. Marriage was good this time around. My new husband had no discernable bad habits and was a really lovable guy.

After the wedding, we did what most couples in America did: we found a place to live and promptly spent ourselves into strangling debt. In very short order, we had a new refrigerator, a "new" second-hand car and a rented place of our own. It was one of the cottages built by my father on Braley Avenue.

Our first son, Terry Thrush, was born in 1956 when we had been married only ten months. As all couples with a new baby discover, an addition to the household is a life-changing event. We had to learn how to do most everything all over again.

We learned to sleep—or rather to get along without it. We learned that money didn't go so far with a new baby to feed. And we also learned that by working together we could even survive a baby crying in the night.

As parents find out, some babies are easier and

some more difficult. Our first took a little more attention. No matter how much work he was to change, feed, and coddle, he was still a delight.

Unlike the shack I lived in with my parents as a child, the one we shared on the avenue named after my father had no rats. But there was something worse than a rat chewing on our lives. It was the gnawing of debt, an evil far worse in many ways than rats. Although my husband worked hard at the local sawmill and I was as frugal as a parent with a new baby could be, bills piled up like leaves in the fall.

As I had learned laying helpless in a hospital bed on more than one occasion with no one to turn to but God, prayer can indeed turn hopeless situations around. Given the limitations of my mortal human eyes, I could not see a way out of our choking debt, so I prayed about it. I asked the Lord who delivered me from polio and saved me from leukemia to get us out.

I prayed and received the answer. Sometimes the Lord doesn't give answers that we want. Or tasks that we think we can accomplish. But when we ask for His advice, we had better be ready to listen.

In biblical times, people faced difficulties and were rewarded for their faith. For a certain widow, the order from above was to go to an empty pot of oil and pour more out. To feed 5,000 people, it was to find a small boy with some fish and bread. For the prophet Elijah, it was to be fed by ravens.

For us at that time, the answer was to tithe. Spend to save? Pay tithe when we were drowning in debt? We couldn't afford to pay attention! But the Lord led. After paying our tithe (and moving back in with my parents), we were able to dig our way out and pay off our bills one dollar at a time. Prayer and tithing saved us from our strangling debt.

TALKING TO A TRUCK

My dream of living in a place where there was little rain and no snow didn't end with my first marriage or die with the debt we had been in. It was alive and well and incubated within. After much discussion, and a promise to move back to Oregon when we retired (a lifetime away at that time), we decided to move to warmer weather with our new baby.

The dream hatched when my husband and I loaded many of our possessions into a trailer made by my dad and headed south. Our goal was the land that, at least for me, flowed with milk and honey. When I consider how few things we owned at the time, I realize how much the Lord has indeed blessed us. The property we had then would fill only a small corner of our garage. How life changes; we think that we need stuff. We don't. The Lord provides.

Later my parents brought the rest of our meager possessions to San Diego in an old truck they bought for fifty dollars. It is amazing how the economy has changed. We routinely put more in our gas tanks now than they spent on this vehicle.

When my parents followed us to San Diego, they found that their old fifty-dollar truck wouldn't cooperate any better than a stubborn mule. With its burden of the rest of our worldly goods, the truck became tired and at times would give up. I remember my mother telling us about sitting on the side of the road while the wayward vehicle was being fixed by my loving father one time too many. After several breakdowns, she finally became so frustrated with it that she got out and looked it squarely in the headlights and had a conversation with it that went something like this:

"If you don't go up that hill and get us to San Diego, it's to the scrap heap with you!" she shouted.

The truck didn't talk back like Balaam's talking donkey of the Bible, it just seemed to go. Apparently it understood the threats as much as an inanimate object can and acted to avoid them. Ultimately we made it to the Promised Land in somewhat less than forty years of wandering through the desert. Interestingly, a little more than forty years after that event, it was time for us to heed the calling and "retire" to the land I promised my husband I would return to in retirement; Oregon. It was to be where we would ultimately build Noah's Ark. And it was the land that, for him, flowed with milk and honey.

THE TUMBLEWEED CHRISTMAS

In late 1956, we found ourselves living in San Diego. It was where we would dwell full time until our "retirement" and ark-building adventure many years later. After Minnesota winters and the rain of the Pacific Northwest, it was paradise. Our first residence there was a rented home in an eight-plex in the Linda Vista community. I took in ironing and cooked for college students while Irvin got a job delivering furniture for the astounding wage of $2 per hour. We found it was just as easy to get into debt in San Diego as it was in Coos Bay, so, we planned for the future by using long-term solutions to difficulties in the present.

With real-estate prices heading skyward in California, it seemed pointless to throw money away on rent. So we decided to buy a house in spite of our income. The dragon of debt was awakened once more as we bought a house with a yard on a lovely canyon in back. Of course, with the house came what seemed a yawning chasm of a mortgage.

I remember trying to sign the papers and couldn't do it the first day. A loan for $12,000 seemed higher than Everest! This was especially true when we had to take steps of $2 per hour to get there. Today most new cars cost twice that much.

As in all things, the Lord led. We prayed and talked, and the next day we signed the mortgage and had a two-bedroom mansion to call home. After spending every penny for the down payment, we didn't have extra to spend on frivolous things. For Christmas we had no money for a tree, let alone presents to put under it. So we made due in old west fashion: we decorated a tumbleweed!

Tumbleweeds are interesting plants. They are full shrubs that grow on a small stalk into a plump round ball. After a period of rapid growth over the winter they turn brown, the root withers and falls off and they have opportunity to populate the world with their children by being blown by the wind as they roll. Such movement spews seed for the next crop.

Before a tumbleweed turns brown and makes its way across the prairie, it is a brilliant green. With deft hands and a pair of scissors, one can shape this marvelous but sticker-filled weed into the shape of a pine, no matter the color. With a 1950s dime's worth of tinsel, our giant tumbleweed became a lovely Christmas tree.

Sometimes the simplest Christmas is the best. The very first was not spent in presence of a decorated tree or even a fancied-up weed from a canyon. It was in a manger on loan from the animals, in a Bethlehem barn. Remembering this Christmas, we were rich with our decorated weed. Christmas remains the commemoration of the birth of Christ, regardless of any pagan contamination of the actual date or the manner in which it is celebrated.

When I think about how we were able to create the

ministry of Noah's Ark, I remember that tumbleweed Christmas. With frugal creativity and some imagination, it is truly amazing what one can accomplish. We learned lessons with tinsel and scissors that year that were never forgotten.

CALIFORNIA DREAMIN'

My dream of California had become reality, but it didn't end with a husband, a child, a house, and a picket fence. I wanted a swimming pool. It was such a privilege to live in a place where one didn't run risk of hypothermia by going outside to check the mail and where skies were blue instead of lead. We had to take the next step.

As a mere serf locked in bondage to our bank for the mortgage and to the Internal Revenue Service for what was left, we had little remaining of our $2 per hour wealth for much more than tithe. The last chapter narrated how lavish at least one Christmas was. How then would we afford the luxury of a swimming pool?

I firmly believe that the Lord rewards hard work. I didn't have more than a high school education and couldn't get much of a job outside of the house. And I had a small child to care for at home, so what could I do to earn more money?

The answer came to me as I was watching my own child. He didn't have playmates, and I had to watch him...I could take care of other kids and babysit while my husband was at work! My mother had moved in down the street and loved to come over to chat.

With advertising by word of mouth, we soon had all the kids we could handle. In short order, I was able to earn more by watching kids than my husband could by moving furniture. After a couple of years, I had saved enough money to build an extra room on our house *and* build a pool!

The lesson of goal setting with the reward of a swimming pool was well learned. Later, when thinking about how we were able to set goals and accomplish them by creating the ministry at Noah's Ark, I can see how the hand of the Lord educated me by allowing me to work hard and save towards an objective earlier in my life. "All things work together for good to them that love God" (Romans 8:28 KJV).

FROM ELECTRICITY TO CLASSIC CARS

When our first child was born, we wanted him to have the best of everything we could afford, just like all parents do. When he was a child, we sometimes didn't have much to give, but we gave we had, and we made due. If money wasn't there for a Christmas tree, we shaped a tumbleweed with scissors and decorated it with ten cents of tinsel from the dime store. When I wanted a pool, I figured out how to make some money and saved it.

For Christmas presents, we sometimes wrapped socks and new clothes. The kids needed clothes and it made Christmas all the more fun. More presents always meant more joy as children unwrapped them. And, every time the little ones opened something, they didn't know if they were going to open a small toy or a pair of socks. When our boys opened something "good" after opening a shirt, the look on their face was priceless!

Shoes were usually hand-me-downs from neighbors or from the second-hand store, and clothes were the same. For a real treat we might get something to wear at FedMart (it was something like Walmart for those of you who don't recall it).

Terry, our first child, showed an early interest in all

things electronic. He was always experimenting with kits from Radio Shack and making things that went "beep" in the backyard. We once got him a chemistry set, which we later regretted. Fortunately for the world, he never became a chemist.

As hobbies sometimes do, electronics became Terry's career. By the time he was nineteen, he decided that college was not for him and he decided to get a job at Sony Corporation in San Diego. After nearly thirty-five years he just retired. We have been fortunate to be able to harness some of his technical abilities in the creation of our displays. Talking mannequins and electronic audiovisual demonstrations could not have leapt to life without his guidance and advice.

During the course of his long tenure at the electronics giant, he had opportunity to set up production lines in several cities in Mexico and travel to Japan frequently. As his career progressed, I would frequently hear him joke, "I can't go any higher in the company without being Japanese."

Traveling was never Terry's passion. But he was a master at another hobby, which would and still does take up much of his time: restoring antique cars.

A few years ago, my husband gave him a 1931 Model A Ford. He lovingly restored every nut and bolt on that old car to put it in showroom condition. He was eventually to win prizes for it and to be elected president of the San Diego Model A Club. It was the same organization that my husband belonged to many years before.

Terry, like my husband Irvin, was good at fixing things. I always say, "If it can be fixed at all, Terry can fix it!" This singular ability to repair things not only helped with our ministry from time to time, it also landed him a wife. When he was a teen, he helped a young lady whose car broke down. She was so impressed with the job he did they started dating and are still married to this day!

Terry and his wife Carol have two children, Norman and Terra. His kids are adults now and have found their own paths to follow in the world. I pray for their safety on their journey and, like all of my family, friends, and enemies, for their salvation. Norman is married to Maritza and has two stunningly beautiful little girls, Loriann and Olivia. Terra lives with a girlfriend in the desert not far from San Diego.

Life for my first son is not without its personal struggles as well. Like many people in America, he bears the battle scars of a sedentary modern lifestyle and diet. Both Terry and his wife Carol have struggles with health. The difficulties of one son fuel the fire of prevention of the other, the doctor, who is developing an educational program, which if employed, will work to prevent many disorders that plague our society before they develop in the first place.

THE CHEMISTRY EXPERIMENT EXPLODES IN A POOL

In the kingdom of suburbia, neighbors rule. Sometimes we are blessed with good neighbors who are our friends forever, and at other times, we suffer the antics of neighbors who are thorns in our sides. Nonetheless, we are directed to love them as ourselves. After we moved into the first house we owned in San Diego, we were delighted to meet the family who lived next door. They took us out to a movie (before as a matter of conviction we stopped going) and had us over for dinner.

As time marched on, their children worked some mischief on my parents' home two doors further down the street. Later on, these same next-door neighbors seemed to blame our kids—primarily Terry, our oldest— for everything that went wrong in the neighborhood. An area of greatest contention, it seemed, was their swimming pool. Although they had a nine-foot-high fence separating our yard from theirs, anything landing in their pool was always the fault of my children.

One day when Terry was about twelve years old, that neighbor's swimming pool mysteriously turned completely black. The neighbor's wife called me up to complain, and the conversation went something like this:

"Your son turned my pool black!" she accused.

"Your pool is black?" I asked.

"Black as midnight, and I know he did it!" She raged.

I was at a loss to explain how my kid could turn an entire pool black. I could understand the random tennis ball found in the pool, but how could a twelve year old turn the entire pool black? So I asked my son, "Terry, did you turn their pool black?"

"Mom," he said innocently without answering, "How could I turn an entire pool black?"

But we had gotten him a chemistry set and forgotten that there was a little experiment that showed kids how to make ink. I never knew he actually did it until many years after my neighbor died.

Even though kids claim to learn "nothing" in school, they certainly do learn. Using grade school mathematics, he expanded the recipe enough to make a swimming pool of ink. He was upset at being accused of always doing something to their pool, so he decided to do something spectacular. I guess once you have the name, you might as well play the game.

Later, when own his own son was small, Terry built a giant kite out of tarpaulin material and PVC pipe that he purchased at Home Depot. It must have been fifteen feet across and had to be held by a ski tow rope. Once when our second son, Jerry, was flying it, it escaped and flew across the Mission Bay in San Diego and headed towards Highway 5. Jerry swam across the bay as fast as he could but still couldn't catch it. If it wasn't for the neighborly actions of a Good Samaritan on the far shore of the bay who caught it before it hit the freeway, I don't know what would have happened.

Love thy neighbor as thyself!

THE HAPPY THRUSH

By the early 1960s we were finally living the American dream. We had a house with a pool, a beautiful but active child, and lived in California near the beach. We didn't have to shovel snow or dress for rain very often, but something was missing from our lives. When our first son, Terry, begged for a brother or sister, we realized that one more child was needed to make our modern family of the sixties complete.

Although we decided to have another baby after our first, nature had other ideas and we had to wait. Sometimes the Lord asks us to be patient. Like little children, we can be impatient. If we learn to linger, sometimes we are well rewarded. My husband and I had to travel eight more years on our pathway of life before another child would come. But, we agree, he was worth it. Without the small seed of an idea from him, there would not have been a Noah's Ark in Winston, Oregon.

At the time I became pregnant again, we had to slow down our babysitting and my mother took an extra job to keep busy. She began to clean house for a Seventh-Day Adventist doctor and his wife. The wife of the doctor she cleaned for introduced me to Eddie Card, who gave me Bible studies.

Although I had a strong faith and I had accepted Jesus into my heart as a small child, I had many questions about theology that no one could seem to answer. There were books in the Bible like Daniel and Revelation that seemed to defy explanation by other churches I had attended.

There was another teaching that I liked about the Adventist denomination. Seventh-Day Adventists teach that we should be committed to treating our own body as a temple and keep it healthy. Given my experience as a youth with my drinking and smoking Adventist friend, I had no idea they were interested in healthy living. When I learned about the well-being emphasis of the church, I learned that the example of my young friend couldn't have been further from the recommendations of the church!

Our second child was born on a Thursday at 7:15 p.m. after a fifteen-minute labor. He was born with lighter complexion than our first child and had platinum hair. When he was delivered, he had a covering, as sometimes babies do, of whitish sloughed skin. With his white hair and white skin, he looked like a little white angel.

We were hoping for a girl that we could name Sally with such fever pitch that we hadn't even considered boys' names. What an error! The Lord had been good and had answered prayers, so why not a prayer for a girl?

But the Lord gives you what you *need*, what the world needs, and not necessarily what you *want*. And the world needed another boy, this boy perhaps. Nonetheless, we still didn't have a name. I doubt that it would be allowed this day in age, but, as we didn't have a name picked out, my benevolent doctor allowed us to take home our new baby without a name on the birth certificate.

After my delivery, I really wanted to go home right away. With my experience of being locked up in hospitals, I was not about to stay one minute longer than needed. I asked to go home on the night of delivery but they wouldn't let me. In the sixties, they often kept women locked in the hospital for nearly a week after delivery. I would have none of that, so, my doctor agreed that if I didn't bleed and I still wanted to go home in the morning, I could.

Sometimes our bodies don't cooperate. The next morning I not only bled, but I hemorrhaged all over the floor in a big puddle. After my long hospitalizations with polio and leukemia, I couldn't let such a trivial matter as a pool of blood deprive me of my path to the hospital exit. So I went to the bathroom, got some towels, dropped to my knees and cleaned up the mess. Every drop! And like a criminal at the scene of the crime, I got rid of all the evidence in a nearby trash bin.

When the doctor came by for his rounds, he asked how I was doing.

"Fine!" I answered cheerily.

"Are you bleeding?" he asked.

"Not right now!" I said happily.

That very day I went home with my new white-haired but unnamed baby boy. I stopped bleeding, and I kept my little floor cleaning secret for many years.

I was reborn in my new faith the same year. To express my new belief, I was baptized a Seventh-Day

Adventist and began attending the Clairemont Adventist fellowship in San Diego.

New faith or not, we still had only a week to name our new baby. Sally, the name we had picked for a girl, just wouldn't do. To solve the matter of name, we decided to see what personality our new little guy had. Babies demonstrate their individuality from the very beginning. As I mentioned earlier, new research seems to indicate that the mother's contentment or lack thereof during pregnancy actually has an effect on the child's development. After getting to know this member of our family, who was born almost fifty years ago, I am certain of it.

Our new baby clearly had a different personality than our first. He didn't cry much and always seemed content. He smiled a lot and was just plain happy. At first, he was the happy baby. Then, we just began to call him Happy.

We had an unusual family. My husband had an uncle with a delightful personality who was named "Joy." Unlike any possible suggestion by his name, Uncle Joy wasn't feminine at all. Like his pioneer father, he made his way in the world living as a "mountain man," hunting, trapping, and panning for gold. You don't get much more masculine than that.

My own brother, named Gaylen, was called "Gay" for short and was one of the happiest men I have ever known. As I mentioned earlier, he wasn't gay by the present definition of the word at all.

Given the family precedent from both sides, we had permission of a sort by virtue of my husband having an uncle named "Joy" and me having a brother named "Gay."

With the personality our new child exhibited, it made sense then to call this new, happy ball of life "Happy." It was, after all, the sixties, when it was in vogue to give babies unusual names. We've known of the names Flower and Sky. Why not Happy or even Happy Joe?

When it came time to fill out the birth certificate, of course it was another matter. I remember the conversation I had with my obstetrician and it went something like this:

"Happy?" Asked Doctor Brown quizzically. "Happy Joe? No way! What if he becomes a doctor?" (Yes, he really said that, and Happy really did become a doctor!)

So it was back to the drawing board. A few more days sealed it. The baby really was happy. Always content. The name stuck. Happy he was.

Our firstborn son, Terry, being eight at the time, wanted a name to rhyme with his and suggested Jerry. This gave us another idea. In a few days, we went back to my obstetrician and asked to name our son Jerry. We still wanted to call him Happy, so the doctor conceded Happy could be recorded as his middle name. Happy stuck as the name he went by until the middle of junior high when he changed to Jerry.

Happy was never afraid to blaze his own trail in life from the time he was very little. Once when he was small, I received a frightening call from our minister's wife that demonstrated this facet of his personality. Our pastor lived down the street and around the corner, on a very busy street that boasted two lanes in either direction and was divided by two sets of double yellow lines.

At this time Happy was about three years old and loved to play by himself. I was working in the kitchen and he was entertaining himself in our backyard, a place safely enclosed by a six-foot-high fence with a latch impossible to reach for such a small child. The call went something like this:

"Hi Shirley! Do you know where your son Happy is?"

"Yes," I answered. "He's playing in my backyard."

"No, he's not," she said.

"Of course he is. I just left him there a few minutes ago." She knew that our yard was surrounded by the fence, which could not be scaled by a three year old.

"No. He's in my living room," she countered.

"What!" I said, as I checked the backyard in a panic. "Where did you find him?"

"Well. I found him in the center of Clairemont Drive waving his arms.

"Clairemont Drive? Whatever was he doing there?" I asked.

"He said he was directing traffic. Just like a policeman"

He has vague memories of getting out of the yard by pushing up on a latch with a long stick to let himself out. Luckily for him, his guardian angel saw fit to tap the pastor's wife on the shoulder and direct her to look out the window at just the right time. Where would any of us be without our guardian angels?

Just the other day, my happy-son-turned-physician told me about a patient he took care of in the Emergency Room. A family member sheepishly pulled him to the side and asked where he had gone to school.

Thinking that the man wanted to know something about his professional qualifications, my son began to tell him where he went to medical school. That was not the information the man wanted. He wanted to know where my son had gone to junior high school. To make a long story short, he was a classmate of Jerry's from a junior high English class and knew my son as "Happy." Happy he was, and Happy he stayed, regardless of the first name on his birth certificate.

SWIMMING WITH SEA TURTLES AND DANCING WITH FLAMINGOS

Those of us with children realize that to know them is to love them. As I think back over the lives of my kids, I can clearly see the hand of God at work in their lives (and mine) as I raised them. When you bring up your brood, they teach you as much as—or perhaps more than—you teach them. I learned many lessons from my offspring. Such instruction could fill volumes; I can only share highlights here.

It is clear to me as a parent that when you have little ones, you are a parent no matter how old you are; and when you have a parent, you are always a child, as long as your parents are alive.

My second son, who is a doctor, told me a story once of a man he pronounced dead in intensive care unit. The man was in his seventies and had been sick for some time with a number of chronic illnesses. After a long hospitalization, he ended up in the intensive care unit, and as a last ditch effort was on the ventilator to support his life. When my son arrived in the intensive care unit to do his best, the gentleman went into cardiac arrest. After working on him for a time, he found there was nothing he could offer and he ultimately pronounced the patient dead.

At the bedside was a very old man with a cane. He appeared to be a robust nonagenarian. He cried profusely and held the bedrail as if it was the rail of a crib. It was as if he were weeping over his lost infant. The older gentleman was the father of the man on the ventilator who had expired. Once a parent you are always a parent.

Our children took different paths in life, and each faced their own dragons in separate forests. We were fortunate that both of our sons had healthy childhoods. As a family, we climbed mountains and traversed valleys together as we found our way in the world. Although our children were separated by eight years and disparate interests, they are, and always will be, bonded by brotherhood and memories of their early childhood.

Some of the many memories they share with fondness are their adventures at Sea World. In the seventies, we believed that the world was a safer place for children and it was more common to leave children to their own devices in public places at earlier ages than we do now.

When Terry was about thirteen or fourteen years old, my sister-in-law Carol (Gay's first wife) and I would drop him off at Sea World for a few hours at a time while we went sport fishing. At the marine park, he was charged with watching his brother and their cousin Angie. Sea World passes were not expensive at the time, so it was an ideal method of giving the kids something to do while we fished. Especially since Sea World was across the street from the sport fishing dock.

We made Sea World trips and sport fishing days a regular part of our life at the time. It would work like this: We would drop the kids at Sea World, fish half the day and return just after noon with a bag of fish, which would feed our family for weeks. It was fun for all and it put meat (well, fish at least) on the table to boot. It was a win-win, catch-catch, sit-sit situation!

As adults, many years later, my sons told me about some of their adventures there. Sea World, like much of the rest of the world at the time, was a simpler place. The marine park was configured differently then. The entrance was graced with great ponds filled with sea turtles, and there was an enclosure deep in the park where they kept flamingos that were not on public display.

One of their favorite activities involved teasing birds. It was not so much the seagulls or pigeons, but their favorite birds to tease were the flamingos. They didn't do it like everyone else at the park though—they did it from inside the cage.

Perhaps the enclosure they got into was a breeding area, or a place for birds recovering from the stress of display or illness, I don't know. At any rate—the kids would sneak through the bushes and climb the fence and get in and run with the big birds.

They loved playing with the creatures. Being territorial, the seemingly enraged avians would chase them around with open beaks and try to bite. It was exciting for the kids, and perhaps it amused the birds as well. "Let's go to the mean birds!" they would say. Apparently it was great fun. I'm just glad they weren't bitten or apprehended by the bird police for their crimes.

We didn't have much money to give them for spending, so they found ways to collect it. They didn't carry out purchases for people or help push old ladies in wheelchairs; they jumped in with the animals for it! It seems that people would throw perfectly good coins into the ponds with the sea turtles. The kids didn't think the reptiles really need the money, and after all, it was just sitting there...so they collected it themselves!

They did it like this: one of them would act as a lookout for Sea World employees while the other jumped in the pool with the turtles and "raked in" the cash. The kids were always afraid the sea creatures would come after them and bite—but they never did. For my sons, the reptiles were just as much fun as the birds—with a cash reward. I think that in this day and age, places like Sea World would take a much dimmer view of kids cavorting with their animals.

THE THING WITH FINS HIDES IN OUR HOUSE

It was clear from the beginning that our second son Jerry, known as a child as "Happy," was a child who marched to the beat of his own drummer and danced to the tune of his own band. Furthermore, he would usually be the one to invent the instruments, design the band uniforms, and write the music for it too.

I was excited to have a second child. Those who know me well know that I love children. Before my second child was born, I babysat a lot. Ultimately, when he was in college, I continued to babysit Sunday mornings at our local Baptist church to have the pleasure of working with kids.

By the time our second baby was six months old, it seemed that he was destined for the extra-large section of clothing stores. He was a pudgy little guy with beautiful rolls of baby fat and a Gerber-baby smile.

I was mortified though when he suddenly and inexplicably began to lose weight. It got worse with time; soon he stopped sitting up, wouldn't hold his rattle anymore, and just seemed to lie there and stare. Without missing a beat, I took my son to our family doctor.

As I had dread diseases of my day, including leukemia and polio, I feared for the worst. I knew from first-hand experience that there were childhood diseases that spat death.

The doctor examined my baby and ran a few tests. In a short time, I was reassured to know that it was wasn't leukemia, but rather diet-induced anemia. It seemed that I, in my maternal inexperience, had added cow's milk too early. With a change in diet, the anemia rapidly resolved and he perked up. He lost the baby fat during that ordeal and has stayed thin ever since. Bullet dodged!

Most babies learn to crawl before they can walk. Some babies work hard to walk at an early age and skip crawling. My son Jerry had a son, Tristan, who was one of those who wouldn't crawl first. He learned to walk by nine months. By ten months he could walk to the cupboard and independently figure out how to open two different styles of child locks. But that's a different story.

Jerry, our happy child, swam and talked before he could walk. As we had a pool that was especially warm in summer months, we took him in from the time he was in diapers. By the time he was a year old, he could crawl everywhere, swim, and talk—but he still couldn't walk.

Under close supervision, we allowed him to float around the pool in a little inner tube. After a few months, he had other ideas about how he wanted to get around the pool. One day he was floating in the pool when he suddenly lifted his arms over his head and went straight down.

Terry, our first son, jumped in and pulled him out. After he was safely on the side of the pool, Happy was one angry twelve month old. He wasn't angry that he got his head wet or went underwater; he was upset that he had been pulled out of the pool. He wanted to be underwater. Ultimately he would go on to become a certified SCUBA diver by the age of fourteen. At that time, fourteen was the earliest that one could earn a such a certificate.

A short time after this episode in the pool, a similar thing happened. As he swam along without his inner tube, he began to bob his head up and say, "Mom!" After a few moments of head bobs and these utterances I developed the idea that he needed help. So I told Terry to jump in and save his brother. Again.

After being pulled out once more, Happy was unhappy. "I was only trying to tell you I am going to swim to the end of the pool," he bellowed. With that he promptly jumped in and swam the entire thirty feet length of the pool. By himself.

As verbal as he was at the time, he made it quite clear that he was going to swim without his inner tube. His improvised baby stroke wouldn't have won him any freestyle competitions, but it did get him across the pool. It was a strange kind of bobbing-grunting-porpoise movement. He would go through the water with his head down—then fling it back to get his mouth out of the water to breathe.

A few years ago he told me about taking care of an elderly man in the ER who knew us as a family for about fifty years. The old man delighted the nurses with stories of the swimming baby who had become the doctor.

Unlike our first son who gravitated towards all things electrical, Jerry was attracted to all things biological. His earliest interest was animals.

He collected them and information about them everywhere he could. In San Diego, if it was alive—or had been at any time in the history of the world (as in the case of fossils)—and could be brought home, he would collect it.

At first it was insects, lizards, and snakes from the backyard. Later he would bring home mice, rabbits and birds, iguanas—you name it. Once, a king snake that he caught crawled into our piano and disappeared. It must have eventually gotten out of the house by itself because we never saw it again.

With all of the animals he brought in the house, I had to draw the line somewhere. I tolerate a lot, but no birds were allowed inside. I hate their flapping wings. Once my father scared me with a chicken—and that was it for me and birds.

Show and tell in my Happy's kindergarten class was always a hoot. The first week of kindergarten he brought a giant toad. The day ended with the teacher standing on a desk and screaming and the kids hopping amok with the rogue amphibian.

In the dark ages before the advice given to Dudley Moore in the movie The Graduate ("plastics" for those of you who haven't seen it), Happy would often take creatures to class in glass jars.

Mixing glass and kindergarteners can cause shattering results. It's especially bad when there are creepy-crawlies inside the glass. Eventually he learned to put his jars in paper bags so there would be no jail break when the glass did.

One day, for the umpteenth time, his jar of show and tell dissolved into shards. And for the zillionth time, he asked his teacher for a new container. By this point this instructor had had enough of his requests for new containers. The conversation went something like this:

"I will not get you a new jar! I've given you a new jar nearly every week, and I just can't do it anymore," said his teacher.

"Well that's okay," he grinned. "I don't mind if a scorpion is loose in your classroom if you don't." He told me he never saw a woman move so fast to get a jar for a child in his life!

There was another instance where he caught and brought some kind of a lungfish home from a swampy area of Mission Bay. He was about six years old and somehow made the identification. I wasn't sure whether to believe him or not, but the next day when the fish completely disappeared, I began to think that his fish story of a little swimmer that could walk on land and survive out of water might be right.

In the morning when we found the tank empty, we searched his room. We also searched the hallway, the bathroom, the living room, and behind the furniture, but—no fish. The front of the closet was clear, but my son knew where the fish would be.

"It has to be in the back of the closet," he announced.

"There is *no* way I'm going to take all that stuff out of that closet. The fish *can't* possibly be in there," I said.

He started to cry that the fish was going to die if we didn't unpack that closet right then. I didn't know what to do. I really didn't want to take all the stuff out of the closet. Fish don't walk. They don't breathe air. And they don't get out of their tanks and play hide-and-seek in closets.

We unpacked the closet. Of course, the fish was there. And it was alive!

Through the years, he managed to bring all manner of creatures to school. There were not only frogs and toads but rattlesnakes (in locked cages) and homing pigeons too. I think the San Diego Unified School District must have changed rules since his time. Probably because of him.

Later we discovered a program at the San Diego Natural History Museum where you could check out animals to take to schools. He would love to check them out, learn all about them, and take them to school to dazzle the other kids.

Still later, when still a child; he began his own natural history museum. Some of the collection still exists here at Noah's Ark. There is an armadillo here; a fox there, and even a full size mount of a 7'6" black bear. Most of the collection items came from family members or were given to him by friends over the years. His love of animals would later be more significant in the development of our ministry theme.

THE HIGH SCHOOL DROPOUT WHO ATTENDED STANFORD

After his adventures wading with sea turtles when Sea World employees turned a blind eye, Jerry continued on his unusual pathway in life. In our family he is still known as the idea person. There are many people in the world who are idea people. Such a person who can incubate and hatch his schemes is rare. Jerry can not only lay ideas, but he can incubate and hatch them as well. We are fortunate to harness his creativity and vision. These aspects of his personality, perhaps in some way inherited from my father, helped to create the ministry at Noah's Ark. Some of his more unusual projects are depicted in the photo section.

When Jerry—still known as Happy at the time—was in the fourth grade, he wanted to play in the school band and was delighted when his aunt loaned him a trumpet. After mastering the basics of the horn, he decided that what he really wanted to play was the violin.

Those of you who have had fourth graders know that sometimes children have whims. They can change interests as frequently as socks. I knew that and wasn't really too excited to have another instrument in the house.

Of all his talents, our second son is also a negotiator: he convinced me that if he could teach himself to play the violin well enough to be accepted into the school orchestra, that I would give him an allowance.

So, as an experiment, I bought him an old fifty-dollar violin. Those of you who are musicians realize that violins can be more, rather than less, difficult to learn. And it's especially hard to teach oneself to play one. So I thought I was pretty safe from having to give an allowance for a long time.

Two weeks later he had taught himself to play the instrument well enough to be in the school orchestra. Ouch! All turned out well. He really wanted the violin, not an allowance—so the allowance was short lived.

He eventually took violin lessons and became quite good. He played first violin in the college orchestra, in at least one community orchestra, and even the electric violin in a group called "The San Diego Gospel Jamboree."

It was a motorcycle that he blames for getting him into medical school though. Here is the story: Jerry was about fourteen years old and wanted a motorbike. After a family tragedy on a motorcycle, I really did *not* think it was a good idea.

I mentioned that Jerry was a negotiator as well as an idea person. Once he has an idea about something he really wants, he goes after it and generally gets it. So, he opened negotiations using the euphemism "mini-bike" for motorcycle. He had a mini-bike that was very small many years before. But that was before someone in the family was killed on a motorcycle. The conversation went something like this:

"Mom, I'd like to get a mini-bike," he announced.

"No," I responded.

"What if I pay for it myself?" he pleaded

"No!"

Now, he's also a thinker, so he contemplated the idea of what parents usually want from their kids. He didn't get into trouble—so staying out of trouble wouldn't help this negotiation. But his grades, though good, weren't fabulous.

"What if I get straight A's?" he queried.

"No."

He had to think a little harder. This was going to be tougher than he thought. I wasn't going to back down. Neither was he of course.

"What if I get straight A's for two quarters in a row?"

Wow. This was getting interesting. A mini-bike isn't a real motorcycle after all. They don't go fast. It wouldn't be on the street. And what are the odds of two quarters of straight A's anyway? I should have thought this much about the violin. I was clearly getting better as a parent and becoming more skilled as a negotiator.

"Okay. Two quarters of straight A's. You pay for it. You got it. But it has to be small."

"No more than 75 cc's," he smiled.

Of course he knew exactly what he wanted. It was more of a small motorcycle than a mini-bike. But I had made the deal and had to keep my end of the bargain when he kept his. He got the motorcycle and learned that it was easy to get straight A's.

I shouldn't have negotiated with him when he wanted to grow his hair long a few years later. Hippies and miscreants had long hair. Street people had long hair. Smokers, rock stars, and alcoholics had long hair.

A son of mine in a church-going family was *not* going to have long hair. So when he asked I was ready.

"I'm sorry. I have to draw the line. There will be no long hair. I want a clean-cut looking son," I said.

"But I'm a straight A student!" he reminded. He was indeed a straight A student by then.

"I know that. Straight A students are clean-cut people," I responded. I wasn't going to let him get me this time.

"We are Christians, right?" he said, seeming to change the subject.

"Of course," I responded.

"Christians follow Jesus, don't they?" he asked.

"Yes," I said. I really didn't know where he was going with this one, but I played along. Christians *are* clean-cut people. I was going to come out on top with this negotiation.

"Jesus had long hair."

Please see the photograph section in the center of the book to see how this debate ultimately ended.

Jerry was a product of the San Diego city school system until he was in the middle of the ninth grade. At that time, a tax initiative took out the program in his school that he attended, called the "Seminar" program. At first he was disappointed, then he became bored, and after a while he decided to take action and look for a different school.

Among the schools he evaluated was a private Christian school called "San Diego Academy." Though admittedly, this one wasn't high on his list, he looked at it because knew some of the kids who attended there from a Christian summer camp he went to.

When he read the literature about the school, he noticed something unusual. It wasn't the Bible classes or the emphasis on faith that caught his eye; it was the fact that they allowed students to obtain full credit for courses by challenging them and taking exams. As usual, this gave him an idea. What if he could simply take some exams and skip two years of school? He could go directly from the middle of the ninth grade to the middle of the eleventh grade. I wasn't so sure about the idea, but when he told me about the amount of money in private school tuition it might save, I started to listen.

I recall the day he presented his idea to the counselor at the school:

"Well," said the counselor, "I know it says that in the book, but no one's actually done it before, that I recall. And students from public schools just don't do as well as our students on exams. Our educational standards are...higher, you know."

"What do I need to do first?" asked my son.

"There's the placement exam. We'll give you a placement exam to see where you stand academically. You have to take the placement exam before we can even think of giving you any wavier exams. But don't get high expectations; most students from public schools don't do so well. "

He gave my son a placement exam a few days later and Jerry scored from the middle of the eleventh grade at lowest to college level at highest. Not bad for a ninth grader! So, Jerry went back to the school counselor and asked to take wavier exams.

"Okay, I took the placement exam, now I'd like to take the wavier exams," he demanded.

"Well, if it says that in our book, I guess we have to give it to you. Which one do you want to take?"

Jerry knew exactly which one he wanted. But it wasn't just one. "I'll take this one, that one, and the other one," he said naming off several courses he wanted to test out of.

"Why don't you do one at a time?" countered the counselor. "But you have to remember one thing."

"What's that?" asked Jerry.

"You won't pass."

Jerry did pass all the wavier exams he took on the first try and transferred from the middle of the ninth grade to the middle of the eleventh and took a high school equivalency test for a safety valve. The next year he was placed in the twelfth-grade Human Physiology class instead of ninth-grade Biology and he was allowed to take both Chorale (an advanced choir elective) and band instead of one or the other and shop. This benevolence of the school would come back to bite him at the end of his senior year. Looking back at his life, I'm sure that he wouldn't want to change anything.

Out of all his achievements in school, he did something in his senior year that, in retrospect, may not have been so politically correct. He feels to this day it was responsible, at least in part, for his leaving high school without graduating.

He always liked to champion causes that he thought he felt were right. So he wrote a research paper for a class exposing the differences in church teachings and school practices in some areas. It was well written for his age, and he was proud of it. Sadly it was not appreciated by all.

When he was finished with it, he gave it to several teachers and the school principal. The school administration was not amused, and, only two weeks before graduation, they sang his praises by giving him a letter that indicated he could not graduate with his class. The letter stated that certain credits (which the administration previously verbally confirmed would be accepted) were not accepted after all. Among those not accepted: physiology would not be accepted for biology, and Chorale (the singing elective and name of the group) would no longer be an adequate substitute for shop.

Jerry was heartbroken. His grade point average was nearly straight A, and he was already accepted into college. Luckily, he had taken a GED high school equivalency exam and the college didn't rescind its acceptance. At the young age of sixteen, he left high school, left home, and went to Loma Linda University at La Sierra Campus (now called La Sierra University), where he attended college.

After a year at college, he decided that because he was taking an overload every quarter, he had enough credits to graduate in only three years. He maintains that graduating early from college was not his plan when he started. During his time in college, he became interested in research, and, although also accepted at Loma Linda University School of Medicine, he decided Stanford was a better fit.

When he was interviewed at Stanford University School of Medicine, they didn't ask if he graduated from high school and he saw no need to tell them. In short, when he was nineteen years old, he matriculated at

Stanford University School of Medicine, having left high school without a diploma only three years before.

It is interesting to note that on his twenty-fifth high school reunion a few years ago, the school presented him with his high school diploma. It seems that after urging from Jerry's former high school classmates, the principal at the time reviewed the school records and disagreed with the school administration for withholding it back in 1981. So now Jerry considers himself a "reformed high school dropout." This reformed high school dropout would ultimately plant the seed of the idea for what was to become Noah's Ark.

OUR MOTORCYCLE GANG MEETS THE HELL'S ANGELS

The Cuban Missile Crisis came and went. McCarthyism sought to stamp out the evil of Communism in the United States, and the Viet Nam conflict ended badly. But the Lord blessed us in our sunny little corner of the world.

Our little patch of paradise in San Diego was a lovely place. We built a greenhouse room around our pool to be able to use it summer and winter, and created other things to delight our kids with pleasures we could never imagine growing up poor, such as a playhouse and a built-in trampoline. And, to top it off, my husband got another job, which paid more than the $2 per hour, so I could give up babysitting and focus on the family.

There were some other things that shaped our life when our children were small and that affected our ability to create the ministry at Noah's Ark. If I can digress once again to that time, I'd like to share some more memories with you.

Back in the late sixties, we had a new child, attended a new church, and were very happy. In spite of this joy of life, I missed some things from my childhood. My father always had a motorcycle, and I longed to ride one again. I also wanted to do some artistic projects to keep myself busy when the kids were in school. So to follow my usual pattern in life, I did something about it.

I decided to do two things when my new baby was three. I was determined to learn to decorate cakes and become licensed to ride motorcycles. I took a class for the cakes, and for the motorcycle, I learned to ride in a dirt lot on a Honda 90. After mastering the 90, I moved up to a Honda 150. The 150 wasn't Honda's best model, and mine seemed to break down rather frequently. I remember times when it would stall and I'd pray, "Lord, please get me home!" I remember once when I uttered such a prayer, a couple from my church happened by with a truck. They lifted my bike up into it and gave me a ride home. How Jesus provides!

After my adventure with the 150, I graduated to more power. I eventually owned a 250, then a 350, and finally a shiny new Honda 360 before I stopped riding. Those bikes were small compared to the super-powered bikes of today, but we all got along with a smaller carbon footprint back then. My family used to tease that as soon as the tires wore out, I would want a new one. Maybe they were right.

I loved the freedom that riding offered and rode all over the place! I dropped Happy off to kindergarten on my motorbike, took it to church, to go shopping, and everywhere! My how fun it was!

In a short time, I bought a leather jacket and leather pants to match and even joined a ladies' riding group. There were others who rode in our family too. My husband had a 1200 cc classic 1964 Harley, and my father loved his own large bike—and used it well into his seventies. Both my husband and I had siblings who rode.

My youngest brother, Gay, had many motorcycles, including a standard "chopper" as well as a three-wheeled one.

Gay loved riding, and eventually became close friends with the president of the San Diego chapter of the Hell's Angels. I knew him too, and, in spite of any reputation his group had, I always thought of him as a guy with a heart of gold inside. My brother never became a member of any motorcycle gang—but I think he always wanted to. Our family members would tease him that he just wasn't bad enough. The mockery was in jest of course, but when we joked with about it, he would always get a faraway look in his eyes and say, "You're probably right." We were a riding family, with practically enough riders to form our own motorcycle gang.

One summer when my youngest son was about seven, I bought matching white helmets and blue jackets for us. We called riding "buzzing" and would "buzz" to the museums, "buzz" to Sea World, and "buzz" to classes at Scripps Institute of Oceanography and many other exciting locations. By this time our first son, Terry, was in his teens and spent more time with his friends and experimenting with electronics in our backyard.

Our riding time as a family was fabulous. Ultimately, I owned five different motorcycles over a period of nine years before abruptly stopping because of a family tragedy on two wheels. The tragedy was to strike a most beloved member of my family.

My brother was deliriously in love with his first wife Carol. He told me about his feelings on many occasions. They had a lovely and beautiful daughter, Angie—now

Angie Cohen, who is a jewel and a delight. She is married to a wonderful and handsome man and presently works in public health in Los Angeles. Gay had a second child, Sean, with Carol. After his birth, my brother was very happy. Sadly, though, Sean passed away in infancy. I do not know the exact cause of his demise, but I know that his loss was hard on both my brother and his wife. Such loss puts a terrible strain on any couple. After Sean's death, my brother's relationship with Carol suffered and they ultimately split up.

After the sad divorce of my brother Gay from his first wife, he began dating again and eventually married another beautiful young lady, Sharon Castle, who he loved very much. They made a handsome couple, and, finally over his previous relationship, he was truly, truly in love once more. He was again as happy as I had ever seen him. My brother had long wavy blond hair, and my new sister-in-law was strikingly attractive and was as beautiful inside as she was on the outside. Their lovely personalities matched their looks, and I thought the chance of them having wonderful children was high. His first daughter was so lovely that it seemed only natural to me that he father more.

Gay was reluctant to have another child for a reason I couldn't comprehend. He kept saying that he was going to die by the time he was thirty. Sometimes, for reasons we don't yet understand, people are right about such prophecies of doom.

In spite of his fears, he must have given in regarding my suggestions for having another child, because a short time later, he and his wife brought a cooing baby girl into the world. Like his first child, she was blond and had big wondering eyes. Her name was Renee (now Renee Castle).

Life was looking up for him. He finally seemed to be over his first wife and was back on his feet financially. He owned a house, had a rental property, and had started a film business, "Forever Films," to capture weddings and other special events on super-8 film. For those of you who remember, super-8 was a quantum leap over regular 8-mm movies because it had real sound recording capabilities.

In addition to movie making and the rental property, he started a limousine business that boasted two limos and a spoof Cadillac hearse from which clients could choose. Being the practical joker he was, he mostly used the hearse for parading about on Halloween with a human skeleton and a coffin that he kept for such spooky-spoof purposes. On his thirtieth birthday, I teased him about being "still alive." When I reminded him that he was living, he got a faraway look in his eyes and said, "I guess you're right." The appearance of his eyes should have been a warning, because, even though he was in the prime of life, tragedy would strike in only a few months.

There are points in time when we wish we could hit rewind like we can on a video-tape machine and do it over. January 18, 1978, was one of those dates for me. I remember every painful detail of that night. It was burned into my memory by events that would wake me from my sleep in the early hours of the next morning, and that would cause sleepless nights for decades to come.

It was Wednesday night and my custom was to ride my motorcycle to prayer meeting at my church. The telephone call from my brother Gay came in the evening when I was not home. He spoke to my husband and asked if I could watch his baby so he could go out with his wife to a memorial party in honor of one of his friends who was thought to be dying. Sadly, I had left for church already and Irvin told him that I couldn't help because I was already gone.

Gay said that he understood and that it was no problem. I learned later that his original plan was to take one of the limousines with his wife to the party. Instead, he left his wife, Sharon, home with the baby, Renee, and went by himself on his motorcycle.

The intoxicated driver who pulled in front of him from a liquor store parking lot that night might have been killed instead by the mass of his limousine had I been able to babysit. Police and eyewitness reports indicate that the truck pulled out rapidly and that he didn't have enough time to react.

Gay was killed by massive head trauma on that tragic night. I don't know if he would have survived had he been wearing a helmet. Helmets do save lives, and his habit was not to wear one. In the old days there was no helmet law in California. Eyewitnesses also reported that on the night of the heartbreak, the drunk driver tried to leave the scene of the crime. My brother's friends apprehended him and forcibly dragged him back to the area to wait for the police.

Ironically my brother's death came on the night of a memorial for a friend of his who was believed to be dying. During the motorcade for his funeral—an event that included about seventy-five motorcycles in procession—there was another tragic accident that caused a death within feet of the vehicle in which we were riding.

During that period, media reports indicated that the Hell's Angels and a rival motorcycle gang, the Mongols, were at war. It seemed they had some disagreements, as such groups often do. A few weeks before my brother's death, family members of the Mongols were killed by a bomb blast at a member's funeral. The killing was all over the news, and, as I recall, some fingers in the press pointed at some out-of-area affiliates of the Hell's Angels as possible suspects.

My son, Jerry, known at the time as "Happy," didn't want get into the limousine because of the events in the media involving the riding groups. He was understandably worried. He read the newspapers on the previous week and knew about the motorcycle gang war and the killings.

My brother's funeral procession was led by a good friend of his who had been the president of a local chapter of the Hell's Angels. He rode his chopper in tandem with another at the head of the motorcade. The next two cars were my brother's limousines in which we, his family, rode. Behind us, motorcycles stretched as far as the eye could see. At the end of the group after the choppers there were even more cars, which we could not appreciate from our vantage point in the limousine.

Suddenly, as we rode toward the place where Gay was to be laid to rest, the convoy was broken. When we glanced out the back window of the limousine, we found that we were followed by only forty or fifty choppers. Behind them, all traffic stopped, and the usually bustling California freeway was dead quiet and devoid of any vehicles at all. In an instant we knew something horrible had happened.

We soon found out what it was, and unfortunately, it was indeed as bad as we thought. One of the bikers riding to the side of the procession to help control traffic was killed. It wasn't at the hands of another motorcycle gang member this time, but rather the carelessness of a driver on the freeway. The motorcycle gang truce held.

More disaster was to follow on the heels of this catastrophe. But tragedy strengthens faith. My faith, tempered with the fire of such misfortune became a ministry. I could have used the fact that I was unable to babysit because I was in church that night as an excuse never to go again. I might have blamed religion and on no account darkened the door of a spiritual meeting place ever again. But instead, I gained strength through my Savior and went on. Jesus is more powerful than any drunk driver can ever be.

THE CURSE OF THE MYSTERY SKULL

I don't believe in curses or voodoo. But I do believe that Satan uses conviction in such things to wield control over people. I also know that the world operates in ways that we still don't completely understand. As I previously indicated, my brother Gay told me that he thought that he would die by the time he was thirty.

Although he did see the beginning of his third decade, he did not live to see his thirty-first birthday. He held fast to the idea that he would die. I don't know exactly what fostered that conviction, but I do know that he also talked about "the curse of the skull" before he died.

In addition to the human skeleton that he kept for Halloween fun with his Cadillac hearse, he had also acquired an ancient-looking human skull that had belonged to another friend of his who was killed in a mysterious accident. The original owner; the one who allegedly found it, had also died suddenly in a strange accident.

The legend associated with the skull indicated that it was originally found in a cave somewhere in Mexico and had some kind of "curse." Whoever owned it seemed to die of a sudden and tragic—if not brutal—accident. It did happen to the first and second owner before my brother, and it was to occur again after my brother's death.

Following the tragic collision that killed Gay, his widow, Sharon, faced new influences in her life and became involved with people who she felt might become dangerous to her and her six month old baby. She decided that she needed to leave town at once to escape them so she could get a fresh start with her child.

I helped her to arrange her affairs and I remember her face as she left town. She trembled and shook. She was tearful and seemed afraid of something, which I think related to some biker "friends" who tried to "help" her after her husband died. She told me a few things, but certainly not the whole story. It never ceases to amaze me how many "friends" will surface to help an attractive woman in need. In her case they were all men; and to me, most, if not all, had patently nefarious intent.

My sister-in-law had an exceptionally tough time of dealing with the death of her spouse. At the conclusion of my brother's funeral, I remember how she gripped the coffin with white knuckles and wouldn't let it go until she was dragged away from it by several strong men. She kept screaming, "No! I can't believe it! No! This isn't happening!" It was heart wrenching.

As she liquidated her property in preparation for leaving the area, the strange skull remained in her possession. She seemed afraid to get rid of it, but could not keep it. I do not know of course, but I suspected that such fear could stem from a deep-seated fear of the "curse."

I finally talked her into disposing of the skull on the morning I took her to the airport. She got rid of it on that very day before boarding her flight. I'm glad she did, because one of my sons wanted it as a curiosity. He indicated that there was no such thing as curses and expressed the notion that if he did not believe in them himself, he would not face any kind of risk. Although I do not believe in curses either, that ugly thing was *not* going to be brought into my house or be in the possession of *anyone* else in my family.

I had prayer with her on the day she left. Her tears fell like rain, and she shook like a willow in a storm. After our prayer, I put her on an airplane with her baby. Unfortunately I never saw her again. Three years later she followed my brother out of this world in a tragic accident of her own.

It seems she was pulling a skier in a boat without a spotter. Reports indicated that she fell out when looking for the downed skier and was hit by the prop of her own vessel. Five days later they found her downstream. I don't believe in curses, but there are those who believe in them in this world because of such events.

We must believe that our Father in Heaven is stronger than any "curse" Satan can invent. The blood of the Lamb was spilled on our planet that we might be unfettered from the chains of evil. No skull from a cave can ever have power over us, yet we bear the responsibility of not letting things that smell of evil through our front door.

Have you ever thought you faced such tragedy in your life that you could not go on? With the help of Jesus, the painful events in my own life strengthened me that I could lend influence to others through my life and the ministry at Noah's Ark. Through the power of the Lamb, with the guidance of the Holy Spirit and the promises of God the Father—you can too!

Me as a girl on my trike

Five on a motorcycle

Sister Kenney
(Photo source: Library of Congress Prints and Photographs Division; New York World-Telegram and the Sun Newspaper Photograph Collection)

The iron lung ward
(Photo source: Food and Drug Administration file photo.)

The iron lung
(Photo source: Centers for Disease Control and Prevention's Public Health Image Library.)

My father's amazing iceboat invention

My family in 1945

My dad on his Harley

Our wedding

Terry and Happy on a Galapagos Tortoise

Terry as a boy

Happy as a boy

Our boys on motorbikes

Jerry, age 16

Gay and Angie on his motorcycle

King's Castle Exhibit (Photo source: Ted Tessner)

Irvin building the bow

Lyne and the curtain

Tom Zoeter and the Laver and Candlestick he built

Cheryl painting tents

Cheryl painting a face

Mural of baby Moses by Cheryl

Mural of journey to Egypt by Cheryl

The bow of our ark

Interior of our ark, panoramic

The galley

The bookstore

Irvin and the ark playhouse

The model Ezekiel Temple

A miniature model from the Holy Land room

Open Microphone Gospel Night

Ivan and Jerry holding mountain dulcimers

Tristan, age 11, giving a lecture

Our scale model of Noah's Ark

The entrance to the Tabernacle

Dressed for a tour

Irvin and the Shofar

The courtyard

Tristan and the Ark of the Covenant

Irvin and the Laver

Terry and the Model A that he restored

The pirate ship that Jerry built

The train under construction on our motorhome

Our motorhome train in a parade
(Photo source: Marc Otto)

The ark vehicle under construction on our motorhome

The ark vehicle completed

Jerry Longbeard and the ark vehicle
(Photo source: Petra LaVictoire)

Tristan, Jerry, Irvin and myself with the ark vehicle

THE SANCTUARY PRAYER THAT STARTED IT ALL

After the tragedy of my brother's death, I turned more of my attention toward reading the Bible. And when my second son, Jerry, left the house for college, I spent even more time studying the Word. I thrived on the most difficult to understand areas. I examined Daniel and went to Daniel seminars to learn more. I reveled in Revelation and attended Revelation retreats to become more educated about eschatology. But there was one area in particular that I had trouble understanding. I didn't completely comprehend the message about the sanctuary.

I knew the sanctuary message held special importance. Lambs, used in the tabernacle of Moses, were obviously symbols of the Messiah, the Lamb of God. I got that part. And it seemed implicit that the ancient Israelites sacrificed them on the altar in the courtyard when they wandered in the wilderness to point forward to Him. But there was something else, something more that I found especially interesting.

The Bible is rich in symbols, and the portion about the sanctuary seemed the ultimate treasure trove of biblical symbols. There was the furniture, including the mysterious golden Ark of the Covenant, the interesting candlestick and the laver, to name a few. And there were other things as well: the colors, the layers of fur, the ritual, and the cloud of fire, which hovered above it all. It was so interesting and mystifying—but what did it all mean?

So I prayed about it. "Lord," I said, "send me someone to teach me the sanctuary message." In answer to my prayer, the Lord sent Pastor Ted Tessner to our church. His favorite topic was "The Gospel in Symbols." He could explain the sanctuary message.

Our new pastor not only taught a sanctuary series, he was to lead our church on a voyage to the Mall in Washington, DC, and to start me on first steps on my journey. It would become an odyssey that would ultimately lead me to create the ministry of Noah's Ark.

We must be careful what we ask for. When I requested knowledge of the sanctuary message, I didn't know I'd be building a full-sized replica and teaching it to people every day. The Lord will open a path for you: it's up to you to take it.

Pastor Tessner spent considerable time teaching his little flock in San Diego about the meaning of the symbols of the sanctuary. After this period of education, he explained his vision of a church project. It was ambitious but ultimately prepared me for what was to be my own calling.

Our church task was to take months of preparation and years of our journey. We didn't know it at the time, but we were to teach God's plan of salvation by constructing a full-sized sanctuary just like the one Moses built and take it on a road trip throughout the United States and into Canada. We made a group decision to go ahead with the idea once our minister presented it. That experience, for our little church, was to be like no other.

When we voted to proceed with the project, there came a strange warning from our minister. Pastor Tessner explained that whenever groups of people worked together to spread the Word of God, Satan was always there, hiding in the shadows, waiting for an opportunity to torment and deter.

Pastor Tessner told us that if we did choose to build it, the devil would give each one of us problems. Like a doctor who explains the potential complications of going ahead with a dangerous surgical procedure, he informed us that the road ahead would be difficult and fraught with potential trouble. With the enormous rewards of a complicated surgery, there were great risks of peril.

After this stern warning, he asked us frankly if we wanted to continue. We answered one and all in the affirmative. Pastor Ted later spoke with us as a group and counseled us as individuals before we proceeded. We indicated that we did want to do this and we were aware of the potential risks.

"Are you certain?" he asked....

Satan wasted no time on me. Shortly after we began, I tripped and broke my arm. Since I couldn't help as much as I would have liked at that time, I donated what money I could to help with the materials. My husband made the ticket booth and enjoyed doing it. If he only knew then he'd be making so many similar things a few years later, I'm not sure he would have been as enthusiastic.

To make matters worse for me at the time, my own mother's forgetfulness increased and she was diagnosed with Alzheimer's disease. In short order, she sustained a fall and broke a hip. Helping her through surgery and a prolonged recovery took more of my time away from our project. Eventually my mother died while the venture was ongoing. It was a hard time for me, but I was consoled by the worthy nature of the project, and when my mother passed on, I was reassured by the knowledge that she maintained a life-long steadfast belief in Jesus.

THE REWARD OF THE KING'S CASTLE

As soon as we completed the life-sized model of the tabernacle of Moses, our first presentation was at the Del Mar fairgrounds in San Diego County. It was an electrifying time. Finally, all of the hard work of planning, building, sewing, and creating paid off, and we were able to open the exhibit to the general public.

Most of us took turns being tour guides and leading people on the fascinating excursion through the life-size model sanctuary. We were able to present biblical history and the symbols that pointed to the ultimate sacrifice Jesus made on our behalf. It was so exciting!

I recall one early experience as a tour guide that had a profound effect on me. I had just given a tour when a man told a friend of mine that he wanted to become a Christian and live for the Lord. He accepted Jesus as his personal Savior right then and there. Although he wasn't working at the time, God touched his life and he became employed. He later returned to the church and gave the pastor a heartfelt thanks offering because he was so happy this had changed his life.

There was another lady in one of my groups who accepted Jesus as her Savior, and her life was changed as well. It was so amazing! When people started coming to Jesus through the project, I made a stronger connection between the sanctuary and salvation! The most exciting thing for me was to talk to the people about the Lord and pray with them and see them rededicating their lives or accepting Jesus as Lord of their life. I never wanted to stop giving tours!

In a period of five years, our group toured with the "King's Castle Exhibit" across the United States and into Canada. On our epic road trip, we set up the display in many places in California, including Loma Linda, Bakersfield, and Manteca. We also traveled with it from Washington State to Washington, DC, and even showed it in Ontario, Canada.

Washington, DC, was an incredible place. We arrived in March, and there was still snow on the ground. It was so cold that we could not set it up on the first day we were there. It was delightful to set it up between the White House and the Washington Monument.

Satan kept us busy while we were there, though. On both Saturdays, the wind and rain blew the courtyard curtains down. There were more days than we could count when we were cold, and some days we were hungry for lack of being able to take breaks and eat.

Our nation's capital is beautiful. If you have never been there, I really encourage you to go. When we were there, the cherry trees were blooming and it was a marvelous sight. Our accommodations were not five-star and we often slept on the floor at various churches.

I remember difficulty sleeping one night in particular. Four of us ladies were sleeping on the floor in a church, and there was a terrible noise that seemed to be a vibration coming through the floor. I finally concluded that it was someone cleaning the floor with some kind of an electric buffer with a bad rattle. I found myself awake late at night wishing they would do the maintenance during the day. I later learned that the noise was the men snoring in the next room.

When we were there, we invited President Clinton and all his staff, but they politely declined, citing that he had sustained a knee injury at that time. If he would have come, I can't help but wonder if his life would have been changed as well. I'm sure the Lord is working harder in his life than Satan with his cleverly orchestrated knee injury.

Tours continued to fascinate me. They were all different. As in the parable where seed was scattered onto good soil and rocks, some people responded to the message, while others did not. There were large tours and small. In a few of the tours I gave, people could not speak English. For these tours, they would bring their own translator.

I was privileged to give the last tour while we were in Washington, DC. There were 250 people in that group. It occurred to me then that perhaps we should have stayed and given more tours. People seemed eager to hear this message of salvation based on biblical history.

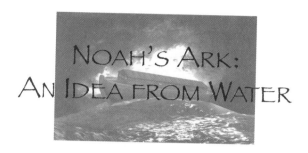

NOAH'S ARK:
AN IDEA FROM WATER

After several years, the "King's Castle" sanctuary tour was drawing to a close and finally I was able to take a break. During this hiatus in my life, I visited my second son, Jerry, who was practicing medicine in southern California. At the time, he had just completed construction on a house in San Diego. His home was built near the beach and designed in a most unusual manner.

Those of you who know him realize that he is creative and different and that he seems to have the unique ability to hatch his schemes. I have previously referred to him as the "idea person." When he built a house, he decided that he had to have a Jacuzzi, an outdoor fireplace, and a giant chess set in stone...on the roof.

So when I was on a break from the King's Castle tour, he invited his father and me to relax with him on his roof deck. His top deck is a peaceful place surrounded by trees, where you can see several beaches with the waves breaking on the shore and miles of coastline. With the foliage surrounding us, it was almost like being a bird in a comfortable nest.

I recall sitting in the Jacuzzi with my husband sitting near us by the fire. The waves beat softly in the distance, and I could hear the far away noises of a city at rest. I began to feel introspective and started to share with him what I was thinking.

"I don't know what to do with my life," I said.

"What do you most like to do?" asked my son. It was his turn to counsel me, as a parent might advise a child.

"I like to give sanctuary tours and tell people about Jesus," I replied.

"Then why don't you build your own sanctuary?" he inquired.

"Oh I couldn't do that!" I immediately countered.

"Why not?" he asked.

"Well, there are several reasons," I responded.

"Such as?"

"I'm too old," I said. "I'd need property," I continued. "And I don't have the money to buy it. I'm not creative, and I can't make things by myself. I'm also not good at leading people either," I argued.

I was on a roll. There was no way I could do it. I had all the answers.

"Those are just details. Those are not excuses," he said.

"But I'm too old," I started again.

"How old was Reagan when he took his first oath of office?" he asked.

"Sixty-nine and a half," I responded.

"And how old was Colonel Sanders when he began to preach the gospel of Kentucky Fried?"

"I don't know, but they say he was about sixty-five or seventy,"

"So they were older than you when they started their projects. How is it then that you're too old?"

"Okay, maybe I'm not too old, but I still don't have the money, don't have the property, and I can't make things," I said.

"And you believe in a God who doesn't provide?"

A few months later, we found a six-acre property across the street from the entrance to the wild animal park in Winston, Oregon. But we couldn't buy it. It was over half a million dollars, way too big, and there was one more thing: we still didn't have any extra money. I remember first telling Jerry about it. Our conversation went something like this:

"An animal park...hmmm," he said. "It sounds like you should just make a building that looks like Noah's Ark and put the sanctuary inside."

"Oh we couldn't do that," I responded.

Jerry ignored my argument and continued: "How wide did you say the sanctuary was?"

"Seventy-five feet," I answered.

"And how wide did the Bible say Noah's Ark was?"

"About seventy-five feet."

"It sounds like the way I do the math, it'll fit," he smiled.

I still don't know exactly how the Lord provided the money to get started. But He did. We got a loan here and there, people who could help started to volunteer to assist by making this or helping with that, and two years later we had built Noah's Ark with a full-sized model inside of the desert sanctuary built by Moses!

The way it came together was nothing short of miraculous: we purchased half the property with loans, and eventually the Lord led us to purchase the other half. Volunteers and helpers came out of the woods, and the project began to take shape. Every step of the way we prayed, and every step of the way prayers were answered.

Remember when the Red Sea parted? Moses lifted his hands, true enough, but Joshua had to wade into the water before it separated. I can't say that I have that kind of faith, but I can safely state that I couldn't see where my foot was going to land every time I took a step. The water was murky, and I certainly didn't see the Red Sea splitting. It was: take a step, ask, receive, and take another step, the whole way.

AN ARMY MARCHES UNDER A DOUBLE RAINBOW

We purchased the land and began to draw plans. Soon our Noah's Ark began to take shape. Soil was moved and compacted, and a colossal pad was formed. Ribs of the building sprang towards the heavens and construction was underway. Even though our version of Noah's Ark didn't take 100 years to build, we only had to ensure that the top was waterproof. During the building process, with the parade of various inspectors, we began to wonder if Noah had to meet city and county code for his unusual structure.

We were required to incorporate into the City of Winston instead of remaining in an unincorporated area. We suspect that such a requirement was designed to increase the tax base for the city. We wondered, did Noah have to do that as well? What building codes did Noah have to deal with? I sometimes asked myself what he had to call his structure to get a permit if one were necessary. I suspect that the county supervisors at his time wouldn't allow him to call it a boat when there was no water anywhere to be seen.

During construction, I also had to keep in mind that if I thought that the City of Winston and the State of Oregon were tough, they weren't so bad. Noah had to deal with a world so evil God was sending a flood to destroy it. On further consideration, Noah had much more to deal with than we did! Perhaps it took him ninety-eight years to get the permits and two years to build.

After the concrete was poured, the steel skeleton of our version of Noah's Ark began to rise high on the horizon. We chose metal because there was a shortage of gopher wood in our area and an excess of termites and moisture.

Early in the course of construction, we became disheartened and discouraged at times. Working with teams of subcontractors and herds of well meaning city and county employees all trying to do their jobs and check the boxes on their forms can be tough as herding cats.

On one of those occasions when we were in the throes of construction, we were graced by a sign in the heavens that heartened us a great deal. As the ribs of our ark rose skyward, something beautiful and unexpected appeared. When we lifted our eyes to the firmament, two rainbows materialized side by side in solemn majesty.

"I have set my bow in the clouds..." (Genesis 9:13 NRSV).

We realized then that this was indeed going to be God's ministry and that we had His blessing.

TWO WEEKS BECOME A YEAR

During the initial phase of our construction, right after our contractor put the sheetrock on the walls, a friend from San Diego indicated she wanted to see our building. She and I were passing through Oregon on a return trip from Auburn, Washington, and she had a little time to stop in and visit. Sometimes prayers are answered by you making an effort. At other times, the answers to prayers just decide to stop in for a while.

The woman was Cheryl Huber, who had also been a tour guide for the "King's Castle," the sanctuary exhibit we built under the direction of Pastor Tessner in San Diego. After Cheryl saw the building, she was moved to stay and help. She indicated that she was planning to go to the Philippines as a missionary but could help for two weeks. We told her we'd be grateful for any help she could give.

She wondered aloud how she could lend a hand, so we asked her what she could do. She told us that she had painted before but had never attempted a mural. She tried, and after a brief mentoring period by another artist, one brushstroke led to another. God guided her hands, and a hidden talent was uncovered! She could paint animals and people and plants and pyramids. She could paint murals!

Days multiplied and months were born. Brush strokes led to figures. Figures led to paintings, and paintings led to murals. Cheryl stayed on and painted the inside of the building for almost a year. Such incredible artwork took form during that time! We never saw anything like it until we visited Italy. Elephants waved their ears, and giraffes stretched their necks. Pandas played, and jaguars stalked. Wood was synthesized in strokes, and the interior of Noah's Ark appeared.

In the back, where the tabernacle of Moses was to be housed, the tents of the children of Israel were pitched by the dozens on the walls and mountains sprang silently into the sky. She filled the canvas of sheetrock with painted desert life, which surrounded the camp of the Israelites. We have never seen such artwork outside of the ceiling of the Sistine Chapel in the Vatican, painted by Michelangelo himself!

The tabernacle display area she painted is like no other that we know of. Cheryl carefully crafted a likeness of Mount Nebo, where Moses died, and painstakingly portrayed Israelites bringing their sacrifices to the tabernacle. In the murals, one can see them with a lamb, a goat, and even turtle doves. There is also a depiction of a man carrying flour and a common priest leading a red heifer.

Superlatives frequently fall from awestruck lips as people enter the magnificent courtyard where the mural stretches seventy-five feet wide and twenty-two feet high! The murals in the building alone are truly something that must really be seen to be appreciated.

After painting the building, the Lord led Cheryl to serve the world in other capacities. There are too many people who helped on the project to name them all. If I have forgotten to list a few, please forgive; my memory isn't what it was when I was a child. Although there were many people who helped make the ark what it is, the talent of Cheryl Huber stands without equal!

The deck and the bow were designed by a boat builder and built by a singles ministry with individuals traveling here from three states to do it. The animals outside were first made by Marian Nance and Elinor Grant. And when they needed restoration this year, they were painstakingly repainted by Mark, Shauna, and Christopher Manfredine, who have also helped us in many other ways over the years.

Lyne Shima and another woman from the church we attended in San Diego sewed the beautiful veils and curtains. God sent so many wonderful talented people. All we needed to do was to ask!

Our white courtyard curtains were sewn by a giant. Although she stood less than five feet tall, Anna Lee Baisden was huge to us. She was efficient, fast, and perfect for the job because she had worked as a tentmaker in the past. Our courtyard curtain was a continuous segment 420 feet long. It encompassed the 75 by 150 foot long courtyard with a thirty-foot long gap for a doorway. How she ever handled those big curtains, I'll never know.

It took two years to build the outer shell of our ark and fill the tabernacle of Moses display area with furniture. We spent the first winter working inside the building wearing our snowsuits because we did not have any heat. It would take another answer to prayer to shed the outfits left over from our motorcycle riding days.

THE MOUNTAIN PRAYER

The Lord gives each one of us a measure of faith and asks us to use it. Faith is something like a muscle, in my opinion. With exercise, it enlarges and is healthy. With disuse, it becomes atrophied and small and doesn't work very well at all. When you don't use your faith, you face the extreme danger of becoming paralyzed and dying a miserable spiritual death. Prayers are the workout in the gym of faith.

One day, while we were working on the inside of our ark before we were open for business, a woman came in and said, "Eight years ago, before you bought this property, I asked a local church to pray for it." She then explained that she had a feeling that it would be used to spread the gospel, that someday there would be a building on this property and that people would come from all over the world to see and hear the gospel and return to their homelands to bring the message back with them.

There is a promise in Matthew 17:20 that indicates that if we have faith as small as a mustard seed, we can claim the promise and ask God to remove a mountain in His name. There was a situation at the ark where there was a mountain that needed to be moved. In faith, I pointed to the mountain and asked God to remove it, and I was amazed at the result. Please let me share it with you.

The construction of our building was complete, but we were still setting up the interior. At that time, we also welcomed another visit from our son, Jerry. When we asked him what he thought of our progress, he indicated that it was great, but one thing needed to be modified. Those of you who know Jerry realize that he frames things in a subtle manner starting with a positive slant. With a little coaxing, I realized his concern was the mountain of dirt left over from construction that partially blocked the view of the ark from the four-lane freeway down the hill. Oops! We had been so focused on the inside of the building at that point we didn't notice what the outside looked like. Sometimes you can be so close to the trees that you have trouble realizing that you are in a forest. For us, this was one of those times. I drove by on the freeway, and to my surprise, there was a mountain of dirt that blocked the view.

Mountains, of course, can be removed by various techniques. Dynamite can do the trick, as can a small army of men armed with shovels or one man with a bulldozer. All techniques for mountain removal, but one, have one common denominator: the requirement for cash. And we were low on currency. Prayer is another technique that can be useful to move mountains, and of all the methods is most cost-effective.

So I told my visiting son that I would ask my Heavenly Father to move it. I prayed the mountain prayer: "I know that faith can move mountains, so Lord, I'm asking for a little help with this one...."

As time marched forward, I began to include my concern regarding the pile of dirt in conversations with others. I recall asking a friend, Elinor Grant, if she knew anyone who could operate heavy earth-moving equipment, and she indicated that her brother, Bob Logan, could operate bulldozers but didn't have any. I realized that it would take more money than we had in savings at that time to rent them, so I filed that piece of information away in my mind, not knowing if it would become useful. Meanwhile, the mountain seemed larger every time I looked at it. After a period, I felt it was sitting there like an elephant in the yard. Something needed to be done about it.

Further inquiry led me to Sam Robinson, another member of our community, who had bulldozers. Without wasting time, I called him and told him what I needed. He indicated that he had two big bulldozers that he would allow us to use gratis—with complimentary diesel, but I would have to pay $300 to get them moved to our building site and find someone who could operate them. At this time in construction, we had reached the bottom of the barrel and didn't have that much left. But by then I had found earth-moving machines and at least one volunteer who could make use of them. The mountain still remained, and I needed someone to smooth out what was left.

To me at that time $300 was also a mountain. It was a mountain of cash. I prayed the faith-can-move-mountains prayer, and the Lord impressed a friend to influence me to put a sign up that said, "Dirt for Sale."

Both my husband and my son Jerry thought that the sign was hilarious. One thing Oregon has no shortage of is dirt. I didn't expect too many takers, but I kept repeating the mantra to myself, "Faith Moves Mountains, Faith Moves Mountains," and I obediently did as the Lord impressed upon me to do, in spite of the heckling jests of my son and husband.

A few days later, another stranger walked onto the construction site and asked about the dirt for sale.

"How much do you want for the pile of dirt for sale?" he asked.

"How much would you like to offer?" I countered.

"How about $300?"

The man who bought our dirt was someone we had never seen before. He was a complete stranger. There was no way he could have known that I needed $300 to get the bulldozers to our site. The earth-moving machines came, and with the kind help of Bob Logan, who operated the large machines lent by the anonymous donor, and the additional help of Bud Essary and Lynden Kruse, heavy machine operators who brought their own smaller bulldozers, the mountain of dirt disappeared.

Faith moves mountains.

THE CHAIR PRAYER

After my prayer moved the mountain of dirt, construction of our ark was speeding along to the degree we could hardly believe it. Cheryl Huber busily painted the beautiful murals, and excitement grew as the artwork took form. During a break one day, she and I had lunch sitting on some tattered chairs in the center of our rather empty restaurant space. As we bowed our heads to give thanks for the meal, I slipped in an extra request. Those of you who have eaten with me know that when I say grace, my prayers often get lengthy.

My philosophy is like this: we're on the phone, and the most powerful, Most High God is on the line. We're thanking Him for the very nutrition that keeps us alive, and we have His attention. He's a busy guy, so I figure that I might just as well use the opportunity to ask a favor or two.

So I prayed the chair prayer, and it went something like this: "Lord, I know You can provide. And I thank You for the food. Now I don't mind sitting on these old, uncomfortable stools, but we're going to have visitors in here soon. It would be nice to have both the comfort of a booth and the mobility of a chair."

If you ask, you receive. David Robinson came in to

introduce himself shortly thereafter and gave us some wonderful seats that are as comfortable as a booth and can be moved around. We have since reupholstered them, and they are just as good as new. A short time later, a nearby hospital closed and a local physician, Dr. John Sproed, was able to get me even more nice chairs for the restaurant. Don't be afraid to pray for the small things as well as the large! Ask…and you shall receive!

An Answer to Prayer on the Curb

It was most exciting to see things come together as a whole as we prepared for our first visitors. To gear up our life-sized tabernacle of Moses for tours, we had to create the furnishings that went in the courtyard and the Holy Place as well as the Most Holy Place. Many people worked on the furniture, both as individuals and teams. My husband was instrumental in supervision and final touches of the various projects and brought them all together in superlative fashion.

The candlestick and the laver were made by Tom Zoeter. I must mention that the candlestick is not only a work of art, it even lights up and twinkles as if lit by a flame! It is fabulous! Stephen Heinrich and Demas Borba made the table of showbred and the altar of incense, and my husband did the final finish work. The altar of incense lights up with "fire" from a faux fire machine when lit by an electric "hot coal." For demonstrations, these pieces of tabernacle furniture really come to life!

The Ark of the Covenant was the most difficult piece and one of the last to be finished. We knew from the beginning that it was going to be tough. It had to be stunningly beautiful and an achievement in carpentry.

Before we built it, I visited a local church and asked someone there if they knew anyone who could make me a model of the Ark of the Covenant. It turned out that there was a woman at the church whose ex-father-in-law had built one for the Seventh-Day Adventist conference in 1985.

She gave me his number, and I called him. Although I hadn't ever met him, he immediately told me he would do it. He only wanted one thing in return. Before he told me what it was, I imagined that perhaps it was recognition or a donation to a favorite charity. His request was far simpler; his only desire was to know what had happened to the Ark of the Covenant model he had made so many years before, which he had donated for teaching purposes.

That was a difficult assignment. To track down a model he had built fifteen years ago and then relinquished to a huge organization was a tall order. I told him I would ask my Heavenly Father and He might lead me to the answer.

The response came sooner than I expected. When we were working in San Diego at my home church on the beautiful colorful curtains, a stranger came in one day and watched us work. He and struck up a conversation, and it went something like this:

"Who is making your Ark of the Covenant model?" he asked.

"It's a man you probably don't know who lives in Oregon. His name is Ivan Graham," I said.

"Ivan Graham!" he exclaimed. "That's the man who built the Ark of the Covenant and the hand-carved angels for the General Conference fifteen years ago!"

I then asked him what had happened to the Ark of the Covenant that Ivan made. He told me that it had been used for so many years for camp meetings, church sessions, and vacation Bible schools that it finally just broke up and they had to throw it away.

"Thank you!" I replied. "Ivan will be so happy to know it was used for a long time in the Lord's work."

So Ivan Graham made us a model of the Ark of the Covenant and delivered it to my house. Interestingly, although I had spoken with him on the phone many times, the first time I met him in person was when he brought me the model of the Ark of the Covenant. I asked him what I owed him, but he indicated it was a gift and he couldn't charge anything for it. After its delivery, my husband Irvin, Ron Parker, and Cheryl Huber added even more detail. It is so beautiful that I hope every reader has a chance to see it in person.

When the model of the Ark of the Covenant was being fabricated the angels on top posed a special problem. I wondered how they should be made. So I did what I usually do in such a situation: I prayed and asked others what to do. My physician son, Jerry who is never without an idea, suggested buying dolls, putting on wings, and spray painting them gold. It sounded like a recipe for a disaster to me, but I decided to pray for someone to do it. Sharon Charles made the two beautiful gold angels for on top of the Ark of the Covenant by doing exactly what my son suggested. It worked fine. And I think she is an angel!

Before Sharon crafted the angels, I gave her some information from the Bible about what they should look like. When she brought them to me I thought they were so beautiful that I started to cry as soon as I saw them. To get correct facial features, she had purchased dolls that were billed as ethnic Jewish dolls. She reasoned that the angels atop the Ark of the Covenant would likely be crafted with features of the people who crafted them. One can purchase all manner of racially diverse dolls these days: Asian dolls, African dolls and Native American dolls—so why not Jewish dolls? With a little effort, she found a pair and put them to good use!

Sharon also made the beautiful clothes and paid meticulous attention to detail to preparing them. She separately glued on each strand of hair and made the wings out of many small feathers. One wing points up and the other is directed down and they face each other—just as described in the Bible.

After the model of the Ark of the Covenant was made, Jerry came to visit with his two-year-old boy. Those of you who knew Tristan when he was a small child are aware that he was extremely active. To give his son something to do when visiting his grandparents at the ark, Jerry suggested and designed a Noah's Ark playhouse. It was eighteen feet long and just tall enough for small children to stand up in. He e-mailed his plans to me, and I liked the idea at once but did not know who I should ask to build it.

I did what I usually do when faced with a dilemma—I prayed. "Lord who do you want to build the Noah's Ark playhouse?" I asked. I was then impressed to call Ivan, the man who built the Ark of the Covenant. So I called him at once and told him about the concept. I indicated to him that I had asked God who should make it and told him his name came up in my mind.

I talked with Ivan Graham about the Noah's Ark playhouse concept and he said he would be here the next week to start. After his visit, he spent another seven days building it. Cheryl Huber painted wood grain on it, and Ron Parker painted a rainbow in the front—just like he painted on the big ark building. The little kids just love it!

When the Noah's Ark playhouse was completed, Elinor Grant kindly painted a picture of a puppy and a kitten on each side peering out of faux portholes. Small children run to play in it every time they come into the ark. The little ones hate to leave here and frequently cry when they have to go.

On another visit, Jerry indicated that he thought we needed to have seating here at the ark for people to relax on that would look rustic, like Noah might have built. He was worried that our furnishings were a little mismatched. As we drove him back from the airport in Eugene on a visit he mentioned this new, but sorely needed, idea. I told him that his concept was very nice but I didn't see how we could possibly find any such furniture even if it was priced within our ability to obtain. Sometimes his mind is in overdrive and he has too many ideas. This was one of those times. Another good thought perhaps—but where in the world would we get log furniture?

While I was busy filing his latest thought, I explained that we needed to pick up some food for the restaurant at Costco. When we stopped at Costco, there on the curb was an entire display of log furniture that was perfect for Noah's Ark. We made the purchase, and they were delivered from Eugene the next day. Answers to prayers sometimes appear on the curb right in front of you.

After we had log furniture, like Noah might have made, Jerry wondered aloud that we should have a wood stove for people to sit by. "Wouldn't Noah have had a stove?" he asked one day.

We don't know if Noah had one in his ark, but in Oregon where it rains all the time and where there are more cold days in the winter than warm ones, *we* sure needed one.

The Winston fire code doesn't allow one here in the building as is, so I prayed and asked God to help. I went to Walmart and walked by an electric stove that looked like a wood-burning stove. It was perfect but didn't have a price on it so I had to flag down an associate.

The clerk said, "This is on sale. Shall I see how much it is?"

"Absolutely," I replied.

It was a deal at $69, so I put it in my cart. I know someone in California who bought one almost exactly like it from a fireplace store for $700. He wished he would have been able to find the same deal. I wonder, does prayer help find deals too?

There was another thing that Jerry was concerned about from the start. He pestered me from the beginning to paint the inside sheet rock and make it look like timber. At first, I didn't think it would really work well enough to pull off the illusion of a wooden interior. But ultimately we did it. Cheryl Huber covered the walls in wood grain, and later, my contractor Scott Gober continued the work and did the steel beams so the entire front of the Noah's Ark restaurant and book store now look like it is made of gopher wood! Many people walk in and can't tell that the beams overhead aren't made from trees.

I must also give credit to Gail Harper. Gail saw the newspaper article about the small tabernacle of Moses that Irvin made, and it mentioned the fact that we were preparing to build a building to hold a full-size tabernacle. She called and said she had a small model tabernacle and had been giving lectures on the subject for years. She is now one of our tour guides for special events!

There was much help the first few years and many answered prayers. Some prayers were answered on the curb, as for the log furniture at Costco; others appeared in store aisles, and still others simply walked in the front door. All those individuals who lent a hand were much appreciated! But we know that prayer was the common denominator.

We opened the end of August 2000 as "Ancient Arks and Temples Inc." but people could not relate to it and started calling us "Noah's Ark." So ultimately we changed our name to just plain "Noah's Ark."

NO MORE SNOWSUITS

Before we opened, we worked very hard to make it happen. When it was hot, we worked in shorts. If it was cold, we bundled up the best we could in our old snow-suits which we used to wear when we rode motorcycles in the winter. We spent every extra dime we had on the project, and still there didn't seem to be enough.

On Sundays at this time, Angie Schulz and her husband would bring us a big box of food, which would last all week. During this period, she also helped us with the considerable sewing that needed to be done. Scott Munion brought us cases of vegetarian chili, and another woman brought us a 100-pound bag of potatoes. Every little bit was appreciated and helped to fuel our progress as well as our morale.

Jim and Ingrid Singer called us after hearing about our project. They said simply: "We are coming to help." After they arrived, they asked me what I needed. I explained that I needed the laver to be built. The concept of a laver was difficult to describe, so I showed him a picture of one. After a few days, Jim introduced us to Tom Zoeter and his wife. Tom made the laver as well as the candlestick. It still amazes me how God brought this all together. We just had to start walking and claiming promises just like Joshua did when he walked into the Red Sea.

When we were building, we learned many things about doing business and opening a restaurant. We constructed our building one item at a time, not really knowing how we were going to fund or build the next phase. But the Lord provided. When we were working on our kitchen, we learned that the State of Oregon doesn't allow cooking in a kitchen with a concrete floor. The next thing I knew, a kind man by the name of Charles Hansen had brought his father in and they begun laying commercial tile for us right where we needed it. It was yet another miracle of construction.

As time went on, Charles Hansen brought his son to Noah's Ark for Bible studies. He always came early and, as my custom was, I fed him and all the other early birds some homemade soup and bread. A few months later, I was invited to the baptism of Charles' son. Perhaps the old saying, "A way to a man's heart is through his stomach," is true!

With all the help and encouragement from family, friends, and good samaritan strangers, we remained operational. In the early days of our ministry, Noah's Ark wasn't as complete as it is now. And, as with the period during early construction, we did without a lot. Shortly after we opened, a man named Jack Ivy took the tour in the back. At the conclusion of the tour, he asked me a rhetorical question:

"You don't have any heat in this building, do you?" he asked.

"I know it's cold, but I'm starting to talk to my Heavenly Father about it," I said, regretfully.

"I'm a retired heating and air-conditioning man and will do it for you," he replied.

Wow! That was an answer to a prayer we didn't even have the nerve to pray! God had been so good—we were thankful to just have the snowsuits. So Jack Ivy installed the heaters, and we are now able to walk around without snow gear!

I did not ask God for air conditioning either, but Jack installed an air-conditioning system while he was at it. I think that it is important to remember that when we ask God for something, He gives us more than we can ever ask or even think to ask. Heat and air conditioning! Before we prayed!

FROM TV TO LIGHTNING BOLTS

Shortly after our grand opening, I was invited to Illinois to share the ark on a talk show broadcast on the Three Angels Broadcasting Network. I had never been on television before and didn't want to do it unless someone would go with me. My husband had to stay and man the ship, so Jerry agreed to fly from California to Illinois to offer his support and appear on the show with me.

I must divulge a secret here: The restaurant business was as new to me as being on TV. I was by that time nearly seventy, and I had never run a public business or so much as worked in a restaurant before. And now I had built one. But as my son would remind me, Moses never walked through an ocean before either.

I was delighted when I received a call out of the blue after the broadcast from a lady who had operated restaurants as a career. Her name was Marie Eldridge, and she came from over 100 miles away and offered to teach me to cook restaurant style. She stayed a while and shared some great tips. What a blessing!

Another call came in from a retired electrician 300 miles away. He offered to help as well and ultimately drove the 600-mile round trip in order to stay three weeks and volunteer his time to do wiring. This retired electrician was the one who connected our audiovisual demonstration of lightning on Mt. Sinai. The Ten Commandments were now lit up, and we had lightning to go with the thunder of God's voice on the recording. From TV to lightning bolts! What could be next?

THE MODEL ARK FLOATS!

Many visitors ask about Noah's Ark when they come in. After all, our building was designed to look like Noah's Ark. Popular demand required yet another model—one depicting what scholars feel such a vessel might have actually looked like. We considered this for several years, but it wasn't until an interesting young gentleman entered our ark and made a declaration that we seriously worked on it.

A youthful man walked in one day and announced that he had an unusual donation. He said that he had been saving small plastic animals since he was a small child and he did not know what to do with his collection. He did not know what to do with them, that is, until he came into Noah's Ark. He said he would go back to California and send them to us in memory of his mother. He indicated that he would give them to us if we could have someone build a Noah's Ark to scale for the animals. Of course, that was a request that could not be ignored with such a gift. And we wanted to have such a display. It was only a matter of time...

A friend and I categorized the toy animals and put them in a box by pairs and size right away, but it wasn't until Bill Hughes, a retired minister, built our model

Noah's Ark in 2004 that they had a home. I prayed for three-and-a-half years before God sent him to make it. This taught me the value of persistence in prayer. It was so exciting to see him make the model of Noah's Ark to the scale of the animals. God *does* answer prayers, but they aren't always answered in your timetable. So keep on praying!

After Bill Hughes built the scale model of Noah's Ark in 2004, one of our cooks, who was also a tattoo artist, meticulously painted wood grain patterns on it, and Irvin carefully set up the animals. Children of all ages continue to enjoy this model every day. Bill has since passed on, but I think that someday he will learn just how much joy he brought to many people with his model Noah's Ark.

For us, building our Noah's Ark remained a little like crossing the Red Sea. Although I mentioned it earlier, I must repeat it because this metaphor always gave us such strength. I understand that the water parted before the Israelites when Moses held up his hands, but Joshua had to wade in first. We sometimes waded in up to our neck before it started to separate with this project. The deeper we went, the more the waters parted. We're still wading, and the water is still receding!

A TATTOO ARTIST TO THE RESCUE

In 2002, Jerry came to visit again and saw our "education room" where we were storing some miniature dioramas and models. Seeing the disorganized Holy Land models, he developed the idea for a contiguous scene depicting the journey of the life of Christ. He suggested that we should place them on the floor, wall to wall, positioned on white sand in proper order to depict the journey of Jesus on earth. We had the models, and they were, after all, just sitting there. The job was too big for me and too small for my husband. So I did what I always do. I prayed for my Father in Heaven to send someone. I prayed, and shortly thereafter, a couple of elders from the local Latter Day Saints church walked right through the door and asked if I needed help.

"Do I need help?" I asked. "I sure do! Come on in. Do I ever have a job for you!"

The young men created the diorama, but they felt the walls needed to be painted to look like the desert to lend a nicer effect. With every step comes another. When we wade in more, the water separates further.

The room already had a beautiful three-dimensional display of the sanctuary of Moses with mountains on one wall. I prayed a similar prayer to the last one: "Lord, you provided the materials for a diorama, and you provided the people to place it. Now, I know it's asking a lot, but how about another artist to finish murals on all of the walls?"

The Lord sent a tattoo artist who came complete with tattoos of her own on both arms. I didn't specify a specific type of artist. But the Lord knew what He was doing when He sent this one. He always does when He sends someone. The artist was delightful, and she could cook, serve, *and* paint murals! The mural she finished on the wall in the diorama room looks the same as the one started by Cheryl nearly ten years ago. It is fabulous!

Our tattoo-muralist-cook did a fantastic job and continued with the mountains just as Cheryl Huber had done on one wall of the diorama room. Their style is so similar that the average observer cannot tell that the walls were painted by two different artists.

The Latter Day Saint elders came back numerous times, sat down with their Bible, and spent more than five hours creating the story of Jesus in miniature. It spans the time from just before He was born until His ascension. Like so many other things here, it must be seen to be truly appreciated.

Our tattoo artist also tattooed (well, painted) the walls in the Ezekiel Temple room. In it she completed a five-wall mural (the ceiling is done as well), which creates just the right environment for the display. Many think it is even more incredible than the first room that she painted. People who see her murals are amazed at the detail she put into the work. Right up to the fluffy white clouds on the ceiling!

Every wall of murals has its own story to tell here at Noah's Ark. Some were painted by Cheryl, and some by our tattoo-artist-muralist. Likewise, the wood-grain art was painted by numerous people. But, like the entirety of the Bible that was written by many authors, the Master's hand remains behind it all!

Ezekiel's Temple Is Sent From Above

The tabernacle of Moses wasn't the only tabernacle mentioned in the Bible. It was, of course, the first, and the most famous. Solomon's temple was perhaps the most ornate, but there are others that must be discussed in any discourse of biblical tabernacles and presented in any educational facility that features them.

The temple presented by Ezekiel was notable because many theologians agree it was to be the last historical ancient temple built by the Israelites. In fact, this temple, if built, would no doubt have been the one Jesus Christ would have worshipped in when He walked the earth two thousand years ago. Historically it was important because it was to replace Solomon's temple that was destroyed in 586 BC.

In the Bible, Ezekiel chapters forty through forty eight depict the vision of the temple and city, which would have completed the return of God's glory during the first coming of Jesus Christ. The name of the city where it was to be built translates as "The Lord is there" (Ezekiel 48:35). The eastern gate of Ezekiel's temple was to be kept closed until the Glory of God returned at the time that Jesus Christ was to appear and be received. Experts feel that the Glory of God had left Solomon's temple many years before.

Architecturally speaking, Ezekiel's temple was interesting because it was based on a different measurement than most ancient buildings in the area. It was based on a measure larger than a cubit that some call the "royal cubit." The regular or common cubit is understood to be the distance from the tip of a long finger to the elbow, about eighteen inches. Many theologians feel that the royal cubit size was first suggested in Ezekiel 40:5, that it was to be the measure of the Ezekiel temple, and that it measured about twenty-one inches long. The chart below compares the size of Solomon's temple, as described in 1 Kings 6:2 and 2 Chronicles 3:1-4, with that of the proposed temple of the vision described in Ezekiel chapter forty.

Solomon's Standard Cubit	Ezekiel's Royal Cubit
18 inches per cubit	21 inches per cubit

Temple Comparison Chart Based on Standard and Royal Cubit Measurements

Dimension	Cubit	Feet, Standard Cubit	Feet, Royal Cubit
Width	20	30	35
Height	30	45	52.5
Length	60	90	105
Porch size	120	180	210

People often ask, why the high porches in Ezekiel's temple? Remember the pillar of fire in the sanctuary of Moses? Many feel that this simulated space allowed figurative room for the fiery cloud that graced the wilderness tabernacle. This high design was also evident in the construction of many houses of worship that followed the Ezekiel temple plans. Some theorize that the stature of that structure may have been an early basis for the lofty structure of many cathedrals that stand today. The Ezekiel temple was surrounded by an inner court measuring 175 feet wide and 350 feet long. The perimeter was one square mile around the temple, and the outer court was five miles square. The gates with their porches leading to the inner court were 105 feet tall. Had it been built, it may have been listed as a wonder of the ancient world.

Ezekiel's temple was never built, and we don't know exactly why to this day. Was it because the people of the time did not have the faith or did not follow God's instructions? The secret lies buried in the sands of time.

Although Ezekiel's temple was not created, the temple that became known as Zerubbabel's temple was constructed in place of Solomon's temple. This edifice later became known as Herod's temple. Some of the people praised God when it was built, but the old men who had seen the glory of Solomon's temple wept at its simplicity.

The King's Castle Exhibit had a nice model of Ezekiel's temple. I felt it was important, so I wanted to display one as well. So I asked the Lord for one. You can guess the result....

Not long after I sent my prayer for such a model, a man called me and said he had studied the Ezekiel temple for thirty years and had made two models of it. He kindly loaned me one of his models until we built our own. I still find it incredible how prayers can be answered. Later, as I mentioned previously, our tattoo-artist-cook painted the walls of our Ezekiel Temple Room, complete with the dome of the rock, the village, and the Kidron valley to make it into a depiction of Jerusalem.

Sometimes miracles are within arm's reach: Bill Hughes, the retired minister who made the small model of Noah's Ark, made all the buildings for our own Ezekiel temple diorama, and my loving husband continued its construction to completion. Sometimes the answer to prayer has been right next to you for fifty years, and you didn't even realize it!

There is one final temple that must also be mentioned in any discussion of important biblical temples. This temple is interesting because it is the one that the Bible indicates must be cleansed before Jesus Christ comes to take us home. It is mentioned in 1 Corinthians 6:19,20.

> "What? know ye not that your body is the temple of the Holy Ghost which is in you, which ye have of God, and ye are not your own? For ye are bought with a price: therefore glorify God in your body, and in your spirit, which are God's" (KJV).

Our body is the temple Jesus wants most to reside in. This is the reason I feel the health message is so important and the reason I'd like to support my physician son in his preventive medicine clinic endeavor.

An Extra Thanks to Those Who Served

I wish to add one more heartfelt thanks to all of you who served our Lord by helping to make this ministry what it is. And you must know that I sent more prayers of gratefulness to our Father in Heaven than you can possibly imagine for your service. Many more volunteers than I can list in a book twice this size came and helped to breathe life into the ministry here at Noah's Ark.

To add a few more names to the long list of those who served, Ed La Plante and Carolyn, Scott, and Dan Gober are among those who I wish to make special mention and give extra thanks. Ed La Plante was helpful with tours when we first opened our doors. Scott and Dan Gober did an incredible job with the construction here, and we wouldn't have the same menus without Carolyn Gober. Any of you who helped and who are not listed by name must know how much I appreciated you too. There were some volunteers who wished to remain anonymous or whom I could not contact before we went to press for permission to include by name. There were others I would have liked to thank but could not because of my own faulty memory. So if you helped and weren't listed, I beg for your forgiveness.

Every day here at Noah's Ark brings happiness to me. I hope you visit, because you are always welcome. If you have something to donate, even if it's a prayer; donations are appreciated too. I hope that you can see in this publication how the Lord has worked in my life and those of my family and our friends and associates to create and expand our ministry here at Noah's Ark.

THE FUTURE VOYAGE OF OUR ARK

I am delighted to have had the opportunity to share with you my personal story and the narrative of the creation of the ministry here at Noah's Ark. As you have read, my own life has not been without its difficulties. I view them as the tempering that fired my own soul and realize that Jesus has held my hand through them all. It is my hope that you visit us here and can experience for yourself biblical history as large as life.

When you come, take the tour of the Ark of the Tabernacle and hear the mechanical priests tell the story of how the ancient Israelites worshipped in the mobile temple they built in the desert thousands of years ago. See the Holy Place and the Most Holy Place and hear our mechanical Moses tell of his voyage in the little ark he was placed in as a baby. See the Noah's Ark room and hear Noah talk about what it was like to build his great vessel and save the animals. By special arrangement, you can also tour displays such as the Ezekiel Temple Room and the Life of Jesus Miniature Room.

Finally, when you are here, I hope you enjoy some healthy food in our fun Noah's Ark family restaurant, Noah's Galley. Keep in mind that we host special events on a regular basis. Here is a list of some of the events at Noah's Ark:

Special Events at Noah's Ark:
Ragtime Music Society musical presentations
Open Microphone gospel music nights
Elvis gospel music programs
Karaoke nights
Bible studies
Health presentations including, "The Behavioral Basis of Disease."
Tabernacle tours
Tabernacle symposiums
The Noah Festival

There is one more question we often hear, which has not yet been answered in this book. That is, "Why haven't you built your Noah's Ark out to the dimensions of the biblical Ark of Noah?"

The main reason, of course, is not our limited vision but rather the cost of the endeavor. A 450-foot-long building carries with it a price tag even longer. And, if you recall, our original mission was to build a building only big enough for the sanctuary.

There is another question we must ask of ourselves before we start hammering away at such a massive project. If we built a building to look like Noah's Ark, which is 450 feet long instead of our present 300 feet, what would we do with all the space? Even if our Noah's Ark is sunk partly into the mountain, it would remain huge.

Jerry, our physician son, has another brilliant idea. He visits frequently and regularly gives health lectures here at Noah's Ark. After practicing emergency medicine for more than twenty years, he has seen first hand the ravages of preventable illness and injury. He teaches a lecture series entitled "The Behavioral Basis of Disease" and feels an expansion project could be used to promote another temple that I mentioned earlier—the temple of the human body.

During his frequent visits, Jerry has watched the area grow from a vantage point that it is difficult for us to have. He sees new signs go up for wineries that we miss because we regularly pass them by. He sees changes in healthcare and primary physician availability and a need for providers in underserved areas. But he sees most a call to educate the public about how to extend their life through behavior modification.

Jerry has also observed what we have done in terms of seminars for people wanting to learn more than they can in an afternoon about the sanctuary. So he has put together a plan to expand the mission of Noah's Ark. This expanded mission may be housed in a larger building designed to look like a full-sized Noah's Ark or in separate buildings. This plan is still in development and its financing is still being studied.

As with our previous plan, it started with a concept. Once the idea was formed, we had only to start wading into the water like Joshua did when the Red Sea split. That is exactly what we are doing now. With each step, the water recedes just a little bit. The bottom is still dark, murky, and slippery, but we march on.

In the past twelve years, we have created a life-sized-recreation of the tabernacle of Moses. We have developed a Noah's Ark theme restaurant and Christian book store. We are presently working on plans to add a health clinic with health care providers as well as family counselors to serve the local area, whether a stand-alone building or an expansion of our existing building. To further promote wellbeing through prevention, we have thrilling plans to open a spa and exercise center. This is an exciting time! Our son, Dr. Jerry Thrush, is now licensed in the state of Oregon and has agreed to be the Medical Director of the Eden Clinic and Spa at Noah's Ark.

As a part of our expansion, we hope to add some accommodations for those wishing to stay over for educational presentations and seminars on health or to study such topics as the sanctuary message in more detail. Our plans call for development of rooms in which people can stay that are decorated with biblical themes, such as a Noah's Ark room festooned with friendly animals and an Adam and Eve honeymoon suite garlanded like a jungle. We also envision an Egypt room for those, like Mary and Joseph, who wish to flee there for a while.

Our area here in Winston is growing and offers much for visitors to experience. In addition to the Winston Wildlife Safari, there are other exciting animal parks in the area, including the West Coast Game Park and the Great Cats Game Park. Although there are many wineries nearby, if you don't drink wine, there are local rivers for rafting and a reservoir for boating and fishing. The visitor to this area should also be aware that we are close to Coos Bay and Bandon with their myriad of coastal activities: dune buggy and quad-racer rentals and deep sea fishing, to name a few.

We are twelve years older than when we began this

project, but we are consoled by the fact that we are at present younger than Moses when he was sent to lead the children of Israel out of Egypt and *much* younger than Noah when he was commanded to build his ark. So we still can't use age as an excuse.

We don't have the funds yet to proceed with our expansion plans. But we do have faith in a God-Who-Provides. Our God is one who cares not only about sparrows that fall but also about paralyzed six year olds and bleeding seven year olds. I will always remember my son's words when I first told him that I didn't have the money for the existing building and life-sized tabernacle of Moses display. He said incredulously, "And you believe in a God who doesn't provide?"

We *do* believe in a God who provides. And we hope you visit us and enjoy a tour or a meal with us in Noah's Galley. When the Noah's Ark expansion project is complete—however it takes form—we hope you come again and again.

If you are interested in watching our project grow, please see our website at www.noahsarkwinston.com. In it you will find a construction information section. There is another tab for fundraising. If you are led to help, please donate what you can.

If you haven't helped with a project like our mission and want to, I have this message for you—you can! If you don't know how, ask God. He might say, "What is in your hand?" It is up to you to open it up and look and see what is inside—and start using it for Him. Do you have a paintbrush in your hand? Is it a piece of wire or a tool? Or are you holding a musical instrument? Or is it an extra dollar for a mission project? Look down again in the hands that God has given you. If nothing is there, perhaps you have time on your hands. If there is truly nothing in your hands, fold them together...and pray.